MW01206002

Project-Based Learning for Teachers of United States History

Shem Fleenor, PhD

1848 Publishing Company

Brooklyn, New York

ISBN: 978-1-951231-26-2

TABLE OF CONTENTS

Introduction

This collection of project-based learning activities for learners of United States History was assembled because I personally needed it. I looked for this book but it did not exist. I thus went ahead and made it for myself and figured that there must be some other teachers scattered across the world wide web looking to inspire their learners with this manner of pedagogy.

It is not hyperbolic to say that society depends on the young. A great education for each and every child is vital, which is another reason why I've compiled this collection of projects. Some of the projects I devised from whole cloth. The best, however, proved to be collaborative and often fleshed out or revised versions of others' projects. The most tedious aspect of crafting this project was hunting down and embedding into the text links to primary sources, secondary sources, music videos, interviews and numerous handouts. But by far the biggest benefit developed and shared here is the integration of pacing guides and detailed rubrics for each project, which both apprises learners of what is expected of them concomitant to freeing the teacher to be an adept project manner – able to devote ample time, energy and attention to any/all learners who genuinely commit to the process of navigating these projects.

Each project in this book contains detailed rubrics meant to guide learners through the process as well as evaluate their performance (according to Common Core and National standards). The suggestion is that learners use the rubrics as guides to successfully navigate their way through projects and to be able to evaluate their peers, which fosters even deeper learning. All of these projects, regardless of the objectives, essential questions, or standards they address, are ultimately devised to help turn the public servant's service into something that can genuinely inspire learners, which helps to foster deep learning. This compilation of activities is, in short, designed to make the teacher's life easier concomitant to fostering deep knowledge, critical thinking abilities, and activism (the enemy of apathy, which is the enemy of empathy) on behalf of learners.

Each teacher/project manager can, of course, decide whether they will or won't make extensive use of peer review. But here's my case for peer review: it is designed to create a sense of community in which those in the community are not simply communicating with some adult who is mostly unilaterally and somewhat arbitrarily assessing judgement. Peer review allows everyone in the community to take part in each community member's education, which creates a culture of accountability to each other (a Civitas).

Project 1

"Marking History, Making History"

Overview: I think this assignment is a good way to start a history course or any lesson on a historical movement. Some learners are not naturally inclined to care about history because they perceive it to be about people and things that happened long ago and are thus no longer relevant. An assignment such as this, however, get learners to view their home and themselves through a historical lens. I suggest having this be an individual (not group) activity.

Objectives: Learners will research the history of their home community or region and use primary source materials to learn about the experiences and perspectives of multiple community members (founders, famous people, controversies, scandals, etc.).

Essential Question: How do learners make history about their home?

Subject: History, Civics, Social Studies

Grade: High School and University

Estimated Time: 5 class sessions (45 – 50-minute classes)

Day 1

The project manager is advised to scaffold the project by giving a tutorial on primary sources. The project manager exhibits primary sources that help to illustrate the history and/or some major events in the project manager's hometown. The manager also introduces the learners to the guiding questions for the project, which are as follows:

- How can we as historians uncover and share stories about our community?
- What are the companies that have and now employ the most people?
- What was and is the primary industry?
- What natural resources and/or attractions are near?

Learners must address the questions above by doing research for the remainder of the period. Learners must also do a quick search of their hometown and jot down some general facts – population, year founded, when founded, under what circumstances, longitude/latitude, etc. Both these tasks need to be completed by the start of Day 2. It is advised that the project manager shows the class the peer-review rubric (see Day 5 below) that will be used to measure their success.

Day 2

Introduce learners to the inverted pyramid and its conceptual framework.

- Most "newsworthy" information at the top – who, what, when, where, how, why.
- Important details, other general info/background info.
- A tail or kicker that ties the information above together in a concise and tidy way.

Learners, using the information they researched on Day 1, use the inverted pyramid to craft a journalistic essay about the history of the learner's hometown.

Day 3

Using the information researched on Day 1 and Day 2, learners will craft a 3-minute presentation (a visual tour) of that person's hometown. Completed presentations must be posted to the Google Classroom stream by 11:59 pm tonight.

Day 4

Presentations.

Day 5

Finish Presentations.

After presentations, learners are to provide at least one peer review according to the following criteria:

Rubric

The presenter posted their presentation to the Google Class stream by 11:59 pm of Day 3. **(0-10 points)**

The presenter was ready, willing, and able to present when it was their turn to present. **(0-10 points)**

The presenter used one image in each slide of their presentation. **(0-5 points)**

The images helped illustrate the text in some way. **(0-5 points)**

The slides were eloquent – i.e., not too much text and easy for the audience to process. **(0-10 points)**

The presenter seemed to have developed deep knowledge of the material – i.e., was not merely reading someone else's writing off a screen. **(0-5 points)**

The presentation was roughly three minutes in length. **(0-5 points)**

The presentation was an adequate visual tour of the presenter's hometown and the presentation helped illuminate some of the major markers of the town's history and cultural development. **(0-5 points)**

The presenter addressed the question: How can we as historians uncover and share stories about our community? **(0-10 points)**

The presenter addressed the question: What are the companies that have and now employ the most people? **(0-10 points)**

The presenter addressed the question: What was and is the primary industry? **(0-10 points)**

The presenter addressed the question: What natural resources and/or attractions are near? **(0-10 points)**

Total score _____

Project 2

"Family History Story Corps"

Overview: I think this assignment is a good way to start a history course or any lesson on a historical movement. I find that learners are often not naturally inclined to care about history because they perceive it to be about people and things that happened long ago and are thus no longer relevant. An assignment such as this, however, get learners to view their family and themselves through a historical lens. I like to think that assignment such as this helps learners to see that history is not past, it's prologue. I highly suggest having this be an individual (not group) activity.

Objectives: Learners will research the history of their family and use primary source materials such as pictures, videos, ephemera, etc. to tell their family history. Learners will also create primary sources by conducting interviews with family members.

Essential Question: How can learners situate their family history into a wider historical narrative?

Subject: History, Public History, Digital History, Digital Humanities, Literature, Civics, Social Studies

Grade: High School and University

Estimated Time: 5 class sessions (45 – 50-minute classes)

Day 1

The project manager is advised to scaffold the assignment by playing some Story Corps interviews from *NPR*. There are thousands of great ones to choose from. Listening to these should give learners an idea of what Story Corps is, what public history is, and provide learners a better understanding of the fact that we are all historical actors and political beings – even those too young to vote. Learners can have part of Day 1 to brainstorm ideas of who they might interview and what questions they might ask. The project manager might suggest to learners that they consider interviewing the eldest member of the family, since that person has the most experience living in the family. Suggest also that learners focus their inquiry into economics, politics, and culture. How did these things impact the trajectory of the family member being interviewed and ultimately the destiny of the family? What are some of their most memorable life events? Why are they so memorable? These are just a few examples of questions that learners might consider deploying in an interview. The project manager is also advised to show learners the rubric (see Day 5) that will be used to evaluate their performance.

Day 2

Learners need to conjure at least twenty questions they can ask, and work on scheduling the interview with a family member (interview needs to be conducted, recorded, and posted to Google Class stream by 11:59 pm of Day 4.

Day 3

Learners must revise their list of questions to the 10 most actionable questions to conduct an interview with (make sure they avoid redundancy). Learners are to practice asking questions with a partner in class and get feedback from that peer about the quality/actionability of the questions. Learners need to have conducted and recorded their interview by the start of Day 4.

Day 4

Introduce learners to the inverted pyramid and its conceptual framework.

- Most "newsworthy" information at the top – who, what, when, where, how, why.
- Important details, other general info/background info.
- A tail or kicker that ties the information above together in a concise and tidy way.

Using the inverted pyramid, learners need to craft a journalistic essay from the material gathered in the research/interview process. Learners must use at least two quotes from the interview in the story. These recorded interviews must be posted to the Google Class stream by 11:59 pm (tonight by midnight). The journalistic essay must also be posted to the Google Class stream by 11:59 pm (tonight by midnight).

Day 5

Learners will provide at least one peer review according to the following criteria:

Rubric

The peer reviewed posted their recorded interview to the Google Class stream by 11:59 pm of Day 4. **(0-10 points)**

The peer reviewed posted their journalistic essay to the Google Class stream by 11:59 pm Day 4. **(0-10 points)**

The story contained at least two quotations. **(0-10 points)**

The story was at least 250 words in length. **(0-10 points)**

The story contained at least two images that helped to illustrate the text. **(0-10 points)**

The essay was free of spelling and grammar errors. **(0-10 points)**

The peer reviewed used the inverted pyramid as a means of organizing their essay. **(0-10 points)**

The interview delved into the economic, political, and cultural events that shaped the interviewees life story/their history. **(0-10 points)**

The interview was at least 3 minutes in length. **(0-10 points)**

The peer reviewed here focused their inquiry into economics, politics, and culture, etc. as a means of situating the personal narrative into a larger historical context. **(0-20 points)**

Total score _____

Project 3

"African-American Christianity and Civil Rights"

Overview: This project traces the long history of how African Americans have used music as a vehicle for communicating beliefs, aspirations, observations, joys, despair, resistance, and more across American history. By examining the nineteenth-century biography of Harriet Tubman, learners will understand how she used spirituals as a secret signal to fugitive slaves on the Underground Railroad. Similar themes and musical traditions grew into what the twentieth century came to know as blues and jazz songs about Jim Crow, World War I, the Great Depression, and World War II. Against this background, learners can consider the significance of the line from "an old Negro spiritual" with which Martin Luther King, Jr. ended his famous "I Have a Dream" speech and the influence of spirituals on organizing for civil rights during the 1940s, 50s, and 60s. This project is designed to engage learners with lyrics, sounds, point of view, close reading, history, culture, media analysis, and performance as part of a rich tapestry of creativity in American history and music.

Objectives: Learners will examine the ways in which music has informed and reflected African-American history and culture. Learners will analyze texts to compare the relationship between music and civil rights over time. Learners will evaluate the extent to which music continues to play a role in the long Civil Rights Movement.

Essential Questions: What role has music played in documenting and reflecting African-American history and culture? To what extent has music inspired political and cultural change in the United States? How has music been connected to civic mindedness and participation and vice versa?

Grade: High School and University

Subject: History, Social Studies, ELA, General Music

Estimated Time: 5 class sessions (45 – 50-minute classes)

Day 1

The project manager is advised to present the following information to the class:

Spirituals arose in the early nineteenth century among African American slaves who had been denied the opportunity to practice traditional African religions for more than a generation and had been compelled to adopt Christianity as a spiritual practice, which allowed slaves to carve out a sanctuary of hop and sense of belonging in the midst of unimaginable degradation and despair. For the most part, slaves were prohibited from forming their own congregations, for fear that they would plot rebellion if allowed to meet on their own. Nonetheless, slaves throughout the South organized what has been called an "invisible institution" by meeting secretly, often at night, to worship together. It was at these meetings that preachers developed the rhythmic, engaging style distinctive of African-American Christianity, and that worshippers developed the spiritual, mixing African performance traditions with hymns from the white churches.

After presenting the information above, the project manager is advised to apprise learners of any and all rubrics that might be used to evaluate their performance during the course of the project (see Day 5). Then explain that scholars have long debated the extent of African influence on the spiritual, but most now trace the "call and response" pattern in which they are typically performed to worship traditions in West Africa. This is a pattern of alternation between the voice of an individual and the voice of the congregation through which individual sorrows, hopes, and joys are shared by the community. In the performance of spirituals, in other words, slaves were able to create a religious refuge from their dehumanizing condition, affirming their humanity as individuals and their support for one another through an act of communal worship. Spirituals also reflect the influence of slavery in their emphasis on traditional Christian themes of salvation, which in this context take on a double meaning. The worshippers sing of their journey toward spiritual freedom through faith, but the song also expresses their hope for physical freedom through God's grace. These two levels of meaning are especially clear in the many spirituals that recount God's deliverance of his chosen people in the Old Testament, in whom African American slaves saw a reflection of their own suffering. Next, show the class a clip of the singing of "Roll Jordan, Roll," from Steve McQueen's *Twelve Years a Slave*: <u>12 Years a Slave 2013 Roll Jordan Roll - YouTube</u>

Next, apprise learners about "Swing Low, Sweet Chariot," which is provided below. Have learners notice the song's call-and-response pattern and reflect on the experience of emerging from the group in the solo lines (in italic) and then feeling the group affirm this individual "testimony" with its response.

"Swing Low, Sweet Chariot"

Swing low, sweet chariot,
Coming for to carry me home.
Swing low, sweet chariot,
Coming for to carry me home.

I looked over Jordan, and what did I see,
Coming for to carry me home?
A band of angels coming after me,
Coming for to carry me home.
Swing low, sweet chariot,
Coming for to carry me home.
Swing low, sweet chariot,
Coming for to carry me home.

If you get there before I do,
Coming for to carry me home,
Tell all my friends I'm coming too,
Coming for to carry me home.

Swing low, sweet chariot,
Coming for to carry me home.
Swing low, sweet chariot,
Coming for to carry me home.

Compel learners to jot down their thoughts and ideas as they relate to the following analysis questions:

- To what extent is this spiritual a song about escaping the physical conditions of slavery? To what extent is it an expression of religious hope and faith?

Day 2

Provide learners with a summary of Sarah H. Bradford (Sarah Hopkins), b. 1818 Harriet, the Moses of Her People. New York: Published for the author by Geo. R. Lockwood and Son, 1886: Summary of Harriet, the Moses of Her People (unc.edu)

Provide learners 15 – 20 minutes to read it. Then have learners read the account of Harriet's own escape from slavery (pages 26-28), where she uses a spiritual to let her fellow slaves know about her secret plans:

When dat ar ole chariot comes,
I'm gwine to lebe you,
I'm boun' for de promised land,
Frien's, I'm gwine to lebe you.

I'm sorry, frien's, to lebe you,
Farewell ! oh, farewell!
But I'll meet you in de mornin',
Farewell! oh, farewell!

I'll meet you in de mornin',
When you reach de promised land;
On de oder side of Jordan,
For I'm boun' for de promised land.

Compel learners to jot down their thoughts and ideas as they relate to the following analysis questions:

- What kind of leave-taking is this song about when it is performed as part of religious worship?
- What is the figurative or coded meaning Harriet communicates to her friends through the song?
- What is the relationship between these two levels of meaning?
- How is Harriet's escape like a passing away from the viewpoint of those she will leave behind?
- How does the song serve to create a bond that will connect her to her friends even after she is gone?

In a later episode (pages 37-38), when Harriet is guiding other slaves to freedom, she uses a spiritual to reassure them that they have eluded a pack of slave hunters:

"Up and down the road she passes to see if the coast is clear, and then to make them certain that it is their leader who is coming, she breaks out into the plaintive strains of the song, forbidden to her people at the South, but which she and her followers delight to sing together:

Oh go down, Moses,
Way down into Egypt's land,
Tell old Pharaoh,
Let my people go.

Oh Pharaoh said he would go cross,
Let my people go,

And don't get lost in de wilderness,
Let my people go.

Oh go down, Moses,
Way down into Egypt's land,
Tell old Pharaoh,
Let my people go.

You may hinder me here, but you can't up dere,
Let my people go,
He sits in de Hebben and answers prayer,
Let my people go!

Oh go down, Moses,
Way down into Egypt's land,
Tell old Pharaoh,
Let my people go."

Compel learners to jot down their thoughts and ideas as they relate to the following analysis questions:

- How does this spiritual fit the circumstances of a narrow escape from slave hunters?
- To what extent is it a signal and celebration of their escape?
- To what extent a prayer of thanks for their escape?

Day 3

The use of spirituals not only in worship but also in the struggle for freedom is a tradition that continued in the Civil Rights Movement of the 1950s and 1960s. As a last step in this survey of the spiritual in African American history, the project manager is advised to have learners look at the conclusion of Martin Luther King, Jr.'s "I Have a Dream Speech,": Martin Luther King - I Have A Dream Speech - August 28, 1963 - YouTube

Pay particular attention to the following:

"So let freedom ring from the prodigious hilltops of New Hampshire.

Let freedom ring from the mighty mountains of New York.

Let freedom ring from the heightening Alleghenies of Pennsylvania.

Let freedom ring from the snow-capped Rockies of Colorado.

Let freedom ring from the curvaceous slopes of California.

But not only that -- let freedom ring from Stone Mountain of Georgia.

Let freedom ring from Lookout Mountain of Tennessee.

Let freedom ring from every hill and molehill of Mississippi -- from every mountainside!

When we let freedom ring, when we let it ring from every village and every hamlet, from every state and every city, we will be able to speed up that day when all of God's children, black men and white men, Jews and Gentiles, Protestants and Catholics, will be able to join hands and sing in the words of the old Negro spiritual, "Free at last, free at last! Thank God Almighty, we are free at last!"

Compel learners to jot down their thoughts and ideas as they pertain to the following:

- How does King use the call-and-response cadences of the spiritual to build his speech? Provide examples.
- What is the figurative meaning behind his literal listing of mountaintops in the United States?
- How does King use the community-building power of the spiritual to rally support for the Civil Rights Movement?
- Who are members of the community that will respond to his call?
- What binds them into a community? Shared experiences? Shared beliefs?
- Explore, too, the part religion plays in this closing gesture of the speech. Is there a religious significance to the communal song Martin Luther King, Jr. envisions?
- Does he impart a religious dimension to the 1963 March on Washington that was the occasion for his speech?
- What is the faith he proclaims here to members of diverse religious denominations as a faith they all share?

Day 4

Break the class into six groups. Distribute to each group slips of paper with the following on it:

- Poor People's Campaign
- Vietnam War Opposition
- March on Washington
- Montgomery Bus Boycott
- The 14th Amendment is passed
- Albany Movement
- *Brown v. Board of Topeka, Kansas*
- Chicago Freedom Movement
- The Supreme Court ruled "separate but equal" laws are legal in the *Plessy v Ferguson* decision
- Bloody Sunday
- The Grandfather Clause, which restricted black voting registration, is repealed
- Birmingham Campaign

Each group is to create an accurate digital timeline that explains what each of the above is/was. Each group is also tasked with finding a song about the civil rights movement that was not covered during the course of this project and explain how that song addresses the Civil Rights Movement. Learners must post their timeline to the Google Class stream by 11:59 pm tonight.

Day 5

The learner will provide peer reviews for groupmates according to the following criteria:

Rubric

The group posted their project to the Google Class stream by 11:59 pm of Day 4. **(0-20 points)**

The peer reviewed here helped contribute to the correct organization of the events into a temporal timeline. **(0-10 points)**

The timeline identified and elaborated why these events were key events in the context of the Civil Rights movement **(0-20 points)**

Each slide in the timeline contained one image related to the issue documented in the timeline. **(0-20 points)**

The peer reviewed here participated in researching and explaining events in the timeline. **(0-10 points)**

The peer reviewed here took part in locating images to add to illustrate events in the timeline. **(0-10 points)**

The peer reviewed here contributed in some way to brainstorming and/or identifying a song having to do with the Civil Rights Movement (and that song was not already covered during the course of this class). **(0-20 points)**

There was some explanation in the project as to how/why that song had some relation or something to say about the civil rights movement. **(0-20 points)**

Total score _____

Project 4

"Native American Contributions to America"

Overview: An ethnocultural community is defined as a group that has one or more shared characteristics. These could be ancestry, language, religion, place of origin, or national identity. The United States is known as a multicultural society made up of various ethnocultural groups. But some of these groups are more heralded in popular culture than others. I recently asked each of my six classes to raise their hands if any of them were Native American. Not one of 180 learners raised their hand. It donned on me that 600 years ago not one ancestor of my learners had arrived on the shores of the Americas. I realized that I needed to create a project that compelled learners to look into this. I suspect that many of these learners are in part Native American, but they just don't, for whatever reason, know about and/or acknowledge that aspect of their identity. This project is designed compel learners to at least recognize the role Native Americans have played in American history and the construction of a very complex and at times conflicted national identity. This project is designed be a group activity with three to six learners per group and groups of six, if possible. This project could, however, work in numerous configurations.

Objectives: Learners will conduct research into the US's history of settlement and colonization, and explore what contributions have been made to the US's history by Native Americans. For example, learners could explore the Seminole, Cherokee, Navajo, Commanche, or hundreds of other American Indian Nations who in some way contributed to the prosperity of the US. Learners will also consider the changes in American policy as a result of these contributions.

Essential Question: What role have native Americans played in the development of the United States into the superpower it was in the late-20th century?

Grade: High School and University

Subject: History, Public History, Digital History, Digital Humanities, Literature, Civics, Social Studies, Philosophy, Cultural Studies, and Theology

Estimated Time: 20 class sessions (45 – 50-minute classes)

Day 1

The project manager is advised to provide an overview of American-Indian history, paying particular attention to the role Native Americans played in major events and movements in American history. Explain to learners that an ethnocultural community or group is defined as a group that has one or more shared characteristics. These could be ancestry, language, religion, place of origin, or national identity. The US is known as a multicultural society made up of various ethnocultural groups. Play the following video for learners: Ken Burns: Confronting America's shameful, violent history makes us stronger as a nation - YouTube.

Then present the class with the research questions below, which are geared to guide learners through the process of the project, especially their end-of-project presentation.

- What struggles and barriers have African Americans in the US had to face over the centuries?
- What struggles and barriers have American women in the US had to face over the centuries?
- What struggles and barriers have Hispanic Americans in the US had to face over the centuries?

- What struggles and barriers have religious minorities in the US had to face over the centuries?
- What struggles and barriers have Native Americans in the US had to face over the centuries?
- How have African Americans been portrayed in the media, particularly in the 20th century? Has this changed in the 21st century? If so, how? If not, why not?
- How have religious minorities (not Christians) been portrayed in the media, particularly in the 20th century? Has this changed in the 21st century? If so, how? If not, why not?
- How have American women been portrayed in the media, particularly in the 20th century? Has this changed in the 21st century? If so, how? If not, why not?
- How have Hispanic Americans been portrayed in the media, particularly in the 20th century? Has this changed in the 21st century? If so, how? If not, why not?
- How have Native Americans been portrayed in the media, particularly in the 20th century? Has this changed in the 21st century? If so, how? If not, why not?
- In what ways have the contributions of your group's American Indian nation changed the culture in the United States?
- What specific impacts have your group's American Indian nation had on American society?
- In what ways has ethnocultural diversity contributed to the U.S.'s national identity?
- How has respect for ethnocultural diversity in the US contributed to respect for other kinds of diversity in the 21st century?
- What systemic barriers do ethnocultural minority groups face in the US in the 21st century, and how can they be overcome?
- What, if any, are the systematic barriers facing your American Indian Nation in American society in the 21st century and how can they be overcome?

Present learners with any rubrics used in the project to evaluate their performance. Then break learners into six groups consisting of four to six groupmates, if possible. Have them divide the questions amongst themselves. Have them exchange contact info and compel them to settle on an American Indian Nation to focus on for the duration of the project by the start of Day 2.

Day 2

The project manager is advised to present learners with definitions of primary and secondary source material and to provide ample examples. Expose learners also to MLA format and show them examples for different sources (such as primary and secondary sources). The Purdue Owl website has several examples the project manager might consider using.

Assuming that learners have access to laptops, each learner needs to find one primary source and one secondary source with which to address one of their research questions (see above). The learner must by the start of Day 3 have annotated the primary and secondary sources they found with a full (5-sentence paragraph) explaining who (1.) wrote the source and where it was published (2.) what the source is about (3.) when the source was published (4.) how the source is of use to the learner in addressing the research question they are tasked with addressing today (5.) why the learner chose this source and not some other options available. The learner must have produced two full MLA citations and annotative paragraphs for the primary source and secondary source by the start of Day 3.

Day 3

Remind learners of the definitions of primary and secondary sources. Provide examples of each. Engage learners by asking them if sources are primary or secondary and encourage them to explain why they answer the way they do. Expose learners again to MLA format and show them examples for different sources (such as primary and secondary sources). Each learner needs to find one primary source and one secondary source with which to address one of their research questions (see above). The learner must by the start of Day 4 have annotated the primary and secondary sources they found with a full (5-sentence paragraph) explaining who (1.) wrote the source and where it was published (2.) what the source is about (3.) when the source was published (4.) how the source is of use to the learner in addressing the research question they are tasked with addressing today (5.) why the learner chose this source and not some other options available. The learner must have produced two full MLA citations and annotative paragraphs for the primary source and secondary source by the start of Day 4.

Day 4

The project manager is advised to expose learners to an annotated bibliography. Explain to them that they will, by the end of the period, have produced something close to an annotated bibliography.

Each learner needs to find one primary source and one secondary source with which to address one of their questions (see above). The learner must by the start of Day 5 have annotated the primary and secondary sources they found with a full (5-sentence paragraph) explaining who (1.) wrote the source and where it was published (2.) what the source is about (3.) when the source was published (4.) how the source is of use to the learner in addressing the research question they are tasked with addressing today (5.) why the learner chose this source and not some other options available. The learner must have produced two full MLA citations and annotative paragraphs for the primary source and secondary source by the start of Day 5. Each of the above sources must also be properly cited in MLA format for each source used by the start of Day 5. Learners must post a digital version of their week's work to Google Class by 11:59 pm tonight.

Day 5

Introduce learners to a thesis statement and how to craft an opening paragraph to a bibliographic essay. Learners are tasked with revising what they produced on Days 1 – 4. They must, by the end of class, write an opening paragraph to their annotated bibliography. The learners must, by the end of class, write a thesis statement and an opening paragraph that includes an outline of how the paper is constructed. Bibliographic essays must be posted to Google Classroom by 11:59 pm tonight.

Day 6

Learners are tasked with conducting at least one peer review according to the following criteria:

Rubric-1

The peer reviewed here posted their project to Google Class by 11:59 pm of Day 5 (the previous night). **(0-10 points)**

The peer reviewed began their annotated bibliography with a clear thesis statement. **(0-5 points)**

The learner peer reviewed outlined the rest of the paper in the opening paragraph, after the thesis statement. **(0-5 points)**

The peer reviewed had three primary sources (actual primary sources). **(0-18 points)**

The peer reviewed had three secondary sources (actual secondary sources). **(0-18 points)**

Source 1 was properly cited according to MLA format. **(0-5 point)**

Source 1 had a paragraph for each source that annotated what the source was about, when the source was published, how the source is/was of use to the learner in terms of addressing the research question(s) the learner was tasked with addressing, why the learner chose this source and not some other options available. **(0-5 points)**

Source 2 was properly cited according to MLA format. **(0-5 point)**

Source 2 had a paragraph for each source that annotated what the source was about, when the source was published, how the source is/was of use to the learner in terms of addressing the research question(s) the learner was tasked with addressing, why the learner chose this source and not some other options available. **(0-5 points)**

Source 3 was properly cited according to MLA format. **(0-5 point)**

Source 3 had a paragraph for each source that annotated what the source was about, when the source was published, how the source is/was of use to the learner in terms of addressing the research question(s) the learner was tasked with addressing, why the learner chose this source and not some other options available. **(0-5 points)**

Source 4 was properly cited according to MLA format. **(0-5 point)**

Source 4 had a paragraph for each source that annotated what the source was about, when the source was published, how the source is/was of use to the learner in terms of addressing the research question(s) the learner was tasked with addressing, why the learner chose this source and not some other options available. **(0-5 points)**

Source 5 was properly cited according to MLA format. **(0-5 point)**

Source 5 had a paragraph for each source that annotated what the source was about, when the source was published, how the source is/was of use to the learner in terms of addressing the research question(s) the learner was tasked with addressing, why the learner chose this source and not some other options available. **(0-5 points)**

Source 6 was properly cited according to MLA format. **(0-5 point)**

Source 6 had a paragraph for each source that annotated what the source was about, when the source was published, how the source is/was of use to the learner in terms of addressing the research question(s) the learner was tasked with addressing, why the learner chose this source and not some other options available. **(0-5 points)**

Total score _____

Day 7

The project manager is advised to show learners Microsoft's PowerPoint Tutorial. Then give one of your own. If learners have experience using other software – Prezi, Google Slides, et cetera, they are free to use that in the construction of the group project. Learners must transform the opening paragraph of their bibliographic essay into two slides in the group project. Each slide must contain an image that helps to illustrate the information in some way.

Day 8

The project manager is advised to provide an example of a poorly constructed PowerPoint presentation. Underscore what is so bad – so ineloquent, etc., about it. Ask if learners have any questions or issues in terms of transforming text into slides in a project. Troubleshoot as needed. Learners are expected to transform information learned from primary-source-1 and secondary-source-1 into two slides in the group project by the end of the period. Each slide must contain an image that helps to illustrate the information in some way.

Day 9

The project manager is advised to show learners part of a Steve Jobs presentation to Apple Shareholders in order to underscore how eloquent and free of text his presentations are. Ask if learners have any questions or issues in terms of transforming text into slides in a project. Troubleshoot as needed. Learners are expected to transform information learned from primary-source-2 and secondary-source-2 into two slides in the group project by the end of the period. Each slide must contain an image that helps to illustrate the information in some way.

Day 10

The project manager is advised to show the class any TED Talk or PPT that makes good use of imagery. Have learners underscore what is so good – so eloquent, etc., about it. Ask if learners have any questions or issues in terms of transforming text into slides in a project. Troubleshoot as needed. Learners are expected to transform information learned from primary-source-3 and secondary-source-3 into two slides in the group project by the end of the period. Each slide must contain an image that helps to illustrate the information in some way.

Day 11

The project manager is advised to show the class any TED Talk or PPT that makes good use of imagery. Have learners underscore what is so good – so eloquent, etc., about it. Ask if learners have any questions or issues in terms of transforming text into slides in a project. Troubleshoot as needed. Learners are expected to transform information learned from primary-source-4 and secondary-source-4 into two slides in the group project by the end of the period. Each slide must contain an image that helps to illustrate the information in some way.

Day 12

The project manager is advised to show the class any TED Talk or PPT that makes good use of imagery. Have learners underscore what is so good – so eloquent, etc., about it. Ask if learners have any questions or issues in terms of transforming text into slides in a project. Troubleshoot as needed. Learners are expected to transform information learned from primary-source-5 and secondary-source-5 into two slides in the group project by the end of the period. Each slide must contain an image that helps to illustrate the information in some way.

Day 13

Reintroduce learners to definitions and examples of primary and secondary sources. Reintroduce learners to MLA format (s). Show another example of an eloquent presentation. Learners are expected spend the duration of the period properly citing their primary and secondary sources according to MLA format. Each learner in the group needs to add the source to a works cited page (or two or three) at the end of the group presentation. The works cited by must be in alphabetical order in the final project.

Day 14

Provide learners the period to tie up any lose ends as far as the construction of the group presentation is concerned.

Day 15

Learners must practice their workflow together so that the presentation seems as seamless and rehearsed as possible. Learners' ought to provide feedback to groupmates. Learners/groupmates ought to receive the feedback from peers good-naturedly. The group assignment must be turned into the Google Classroom stream by 11:59 pm on the eve of Day 16.

Day 16

Learners will conduct at least one peer review of a groupmate according to the following criteria:

Rubric-2

The group's presentation was posted to Google Class by 11:59 pm on the eve of Day 16. **(0-20 points)**

The peer reviewed here added a slide to the group presentation that was derived from the learner's thesis statement and another slide that delved into the learner's scope/objectives. **(0-10 point)**

The peer reviewed here added a slide to the group presentation derived from the learner's first primary source that addressed the research question and another slide derived from the learner's first secondary source that addressed the research question. **(0-10 point)**

The peer reviewed here added a slide to the group presentation derived from the learner's second primary source that addressed the research question and another slide derived from the learner's second secondary source that addressed the research question. **(0-10 point)**

The peer reviewed here added a slide to the group presentation derived from the learner's third primary source that addressed the research question and another slide derived from the learner's third secondary source that addressed the research question. **(0-10 point)**

The peer reviewed here properly cited each primary source according to MLA citation **(0-10 points)**

The peer reviewed here properly cited each secondary source according to MLA citation **(0-10 points)**

The peer reviewed here added their citations to the works cited page in alphabetical order **(0-10 points)**

Total score _____

Day 17

Presentations commence. Groups 1 and 2.

Day 18

Presentations continue. Groups 3 and 4.

Day 19

Presentations conclude. Groups 5 and 6.

Day 20

Learners will conduct at least one peer review of a groupmate according to the following criteria:

Rubric-3

The groupmate was ready to present when assigned. **(0-10 points)**

The groupmates took part in rehearsal on the rehearsal day. **(0-10 points)**

The groupmate seemed to have developed deep knowledge; the peer reviewed was not just reading what someone else had written from the screen at the front of the room, but seemed to know the material well. **(0-10 points)**

The groupmate's presentation was uniform to the rest of the group in terms of color, text, design scheme, elements, etc. In other words, the presentation seemed cohesive and not as though it was a Frankenstein assembled from different parts. The group presentation, in short, looked like a group presentation. **(0-10 points)**

The groupmate's presentation was eloquent – not too much text per slide. **(0-10 points)**

The groupmate used one image in each slide. **(0-10 points)**

Each image used helped to illustrate the textual info. **(0-10 points)**

The textual info helped illustrate the image in some way. **(0-10 points)**

Total score _____

Project 5

"The Blues, African American Poverty, Migration, and Resilience"

Overview: This project is structured around an imagined road trip through Mississippi. Learners will "stop" in two places: Yazoo City, where they will learn about the sorts of natural disasters that periodically devastated already-struggling poor southerners, and Hillhouse, where they will learn about the institution of sharecropping. Learners will study a particular Country Blues song at each "stop" and examine it as a window onto the socioeconomic conditions of the people who created it. Learners will create a scrapbook of their journey, in which they will record and analyze what they have learned about the difficulty of eking out a living in the age of sharecropping. In project, learners look to Muddy Waters and Howlin' Wolf as case studies that illustrate why African Americans left the South in record numbers and how communities came together in new urban environments, often around the sound of the Blues.

Objectives: Upon completion of this project, learners will know how Country Blues music reflected the socioeconomic experiences of southern African Americans in pre-World War II America. Learners will know the basic workings and challenges of the sharecropping system. Learners will know the effects of sharecropping on the daily lives of African-American and white tenant farmers. Learners will know the effects of natural disasters such as river floods on poor southerners in pre-World War II America. Learners will know how the paintings of Jacob Lawrence represented African American life in the South before World War II. Learners will also be able to read song lyrics for information, point of view, and argument, to extrapolate arguments about music by assessing sound, mood, tone, and instrumentation, and to use maps to find locations and construct a logical travel sequence. Upon completion of this project, learners will know factors that prompted African Americans to migrate from the South to northern cities during the Great Migration, including the burdens of the sharecropping economy and racial discrimination. Learners will know how the editors of the *Chicago Defender* newspaper encouraged African Americans in the South to seek relocation. Learners will know songs by Muddy Waters and Howlin' Wolf that reflected and symbolically managed an African-American experience of displacement. Learners will know the role of Chicago's Chess record label in popularizing an Urban Blues sound predicated on electrified instruments and ensemble playing. Learners will be able to discuss figurative and connotative meanings of Blues lyrics portraying the imagery and emotions associated with the experience of the Great Migration. Learners will also be able analyze various accounts of the Great Migration era in different mediums, including photographs, paintings, letters, and census data, determining which details are emphasized in each account.

Essential Questions: How do the Country Blues reflect the challenges of sharecropping, racial injustice, and rural poverty in early twentieth-century African-American life? How did the Great Migration spread Southern culture, helping to give the Blues a central place in American popular music?

Grade: High School and University

Subject: History, Social Studies, ELA, General Music

Estimated Time: 9 class sessions (45 – 50-minute classes)

Day 1

The project manager is advised to begin by presenting the following information to the class:

In the beginning, the Blues was a music performed by poor African Americans for audiences of poor African Americans, and a reflection of their common experiences in the Jim Crow South. The Blues were one of the few forums through which poor, rural African Americans of the late nineteenth and early twentieth centuries could articulate their experiences, attitudes, and emotions. They made music about heartbreak, about the challenges of their lives as sharecroppers, about the relentless Mississippi River floods, about the harsh mastery of white landowners.

After presenting the information above to the class, the project manager is advised to apprise learners of any rubrics that will be used to evaluate their performance during the course of the project. Distribute to learners: Microsoft Word - Song Lyrics.edited.doc (teachrock.wpenginepowered.com)

Then play a clip from Nas on "Bridging the Gap": Bridging the Gap - TeachRock

Then have learners respond the following:

- After listening to the lyrics of this song, what relationship do you think Hip Hop has with the Blues?
- According to Nas, what is the relationship between music and a person's identity — who they are?

Show learners video clip of Howlin' Wolf performing "I'll Be Back Someday" (1964): I'll Be Back Someday - TeachRock

Ask the class to consider just what Nas might have connected with in this music.

Display for the class the quote below, from the 1963 book *Blues People,* by Amiri Baraka (formerly known as LeRoi Jones): "[The Blues] was the history of the Afro-American people as text, as tale, as story, as exposition, narrative… the music was the score, the actually expressed creative orchestration, reflection, of Afro-American life."

Discuss as a class:

- What does Baraka mean in this quote? How does Howlin' Wolf embody this? How would you put Baraka's ideas into your own words?
- Does "Bridging the Gap" support Baraka's thesis? What specific examples can you identify?

Next, explain to learners that in this project they will take an imagined road trip through Mississippi to visit two sites where they will learn about African-American life in the South in the early part of the 20th century, and how that life was reflected in Country Blues music. Learners will visit two stations where they will examine a series of artifacts including film clips, photographs, visual art, and readings. They will answer a series of questions about these artifacts. The stations are:

Station 1: Yazoo City in the Mississippi Delta. Poor southerners, black and white alike, lived in the shadow of natural disaster. Learners will examine songs, paintings, and imagery to learn about the floods, pestilence, and drought that threatened the lives of southern field workers. The resources for this station are:

1. Bessie Smith, "Homeless Blues" (1927): Homeless Blues - TeachRock
2. Charley Patton, "Bol Weavil Blues" (1927): Bo Weavil Blues - TeachRock

3. Son House, "Death Letter Blues" (1968): Death Letter Blues - TeachRock
4. Painting of Jacob Lawrence from the Great Migration Series, Panel 9: The Migration Series, Panel no. 9: They left because the boll weevil had ravaged the cotton crop. | The Phillips Collection
5. Photo of destruction from 1927 Mississippi River flood: MSRiverFlood1927.jpg (934×615) (teachrock.wpenginepowered.com)

Station 2: Hillhouse, Mississippi. Even though slavery was abolished after the Civil War, African-American and white tenant farmers lived a life of grinding poverty under the rules of sharecropping. Learners will examine texts to learn about this economic system. The resources for this station are:

1. "Lightnin' Hopkins, "Cotton" (1959): Cotton - TeachRock
2. "Explanation of Sharecropping handout: Microsoft Word - Sharecropping.edited.doc (teachrock.wpenginepowered.com)
3. *PBS's* "Sharecropping in Mississippi": Sharecropping in Mississippi | American Experience | Official Site | PBS
4. Painting of Jacob Lawrence from the Great Migration Series, Panel17: The Migration Series, Panel no. 17: Tenant farmers received harsh treatment at the hands of planters. | The Phillips Collection
5. Dorothea Lange, Photographs of Sharecroppers: Poor Mother and Children in California (1936): langesharecroppers3.jpg (474×474) (teachrock.wpenginepowered.com)
6. Cotton sharecropper in Greene County, Georgia (1937): langesharecroppers4.jpg (621×469) (teachrock.wpenginepowered.com)
7. Sharecropper's cabin and sharecropper's wife, ten miles south of Jackson, Mississippi (1937): langesharecroppers2.jpg (551×414) (teachrock.wpenginepowered.com)
8. Thirteen-year-old sharecropper near Americus, Georgia (1937): langesharecroppers1.jpg (557×403) (teachrock.wpenginepowered.com)

Explain to learners that after visiting the two stations, they will be asked to create a scrapbook based on their imaginary travels.

Distribute to learners the "Scrapbook Handout": Microsoft Word - Scrapbook Guidelines.edited.doc (teachrock.wpenginepowered.com)

Clarify any part of the assignment that remains unclear to learners. Instruct them to be mindful of these guidelines as they visit the stations. Assign a deadline for completion of the scrapbook.

Divide learners into groups of three or four. Distribute: Microsoft Word - Mapping Your Trip.edited.doc (teachrock.wpenginepowered.com)

Instruct each group to complete the requirements on the handout.

Distribute: Microsoft Word - Questions for Road Trip Stations.edited.doc (teachrock.wpenginepowered.com)

Inform learners that they begin their journey through the stations. In order to accommodate the needs of the classroom, they will not actually follow the route they have planned. Instead, divide groups evenly between the two stations, instructing them to finish the first and then move on to the second. Instruct learners to discuss the questions for each artifact as a group. All learners should take notes on their own copies of the handout. After all groups have visited both stations, reconvene the class as a whole. Discuss the following:

- How do the artifacts you have seen reflect the themes in Baraka's quote and in "Bridging the Gap?"
- How did the Country Blues reflect the experience of African-Americans in the rural South early part of the 20th century?

Day 2

The project manager is advised to present the following information to the class:

In 1941, Alan Lomax and John Work, both musicologists, visited the Stovall Plantation near Clarksdale, Mississippi. Working for Fisk University and the Library of Congress, the scholars were traveling throughout the Mississippi Delta to interview locals and survey musical cultures in rural communities. One of the musicians they recorded at the Stovall Plantation was McKinley Morganfield, an African-American sharecropper who also went by the name "Muddy Waters." Though Muddy worked full-time on the plantation, he also sang and performed the Blues as a solo acoustic guitar player. The songs he recorded for Lomax, with titles such as "I Be's Troubled" and "Burr Clover Farm Blues," came out of a folk tradition through which songs were passed along orally and changed from generation-to-generation. Several of Muddy's songs addressed the worries and struggles of black life and a determination to escape to someplace better. Two years after that first field recording, in 1943, Muddy left his home on the Stovall plantation to live in Chicago. Within a decade of his arrival, he had launched one of the most significant careers of any American Blues artist. Between 1950 and 1958, Muddy Waters had fourteen top-ten songs on the *Billboard* R&B chart and was packing nightclubs with what was by that time an electrified band. In 1963, pianist Otis Spann would introduce him onstage as "the man who brought the Blues from the country to the city," pointing to Muddy's substantial contributions to the evolution of the Blues tradition. Muddy Waters and a multitude of African Americans in the twentieth century left their homes in the South for urban centers across the Northeast, Midwest, and West. This internal dispersion, known as the Great Migration, is the largest internal movement of a population in U.S. history. Between the 1910s and 1970, over six million African Americans from the South headed towards cities including New York, Detroit, Los Angeles, and Chicago, in search of a better life. There were plenty of reasons for leaving, one of which was the prevalence of the sharecropping economy in the rural South. Since Reconstruction, the sharecropping system of agriculture had saddled poor farmers with debt burdens from which they had little hope to recover, keeping many African-American families entrenched in poverty. Meanwhile, as northern cities grew, a range of jobs emerged in factories, service industries, and domestic work. The work was usually hard and unglamorous, and old racial prejudices reappeared in different forms including *de facto* segregation, through which segregation occurred even without legal mandate. Still, these cities seemed far-removed from a region long-connected with generations of virulent racism. Because of American slavery, African Americans had lived as a displaced people. In some ways, the experience of the Great Migration continued this displacement story. The Blues articulated the troubles people faced when uprooting their lives, and allowed migrants a means to connect as they struggled to survive in northern cities. When Muddy Waters sang "I Feel Like Going Home," one of the first songs he recorded in Chicago, or when Howlin' Wolf bellowed "Smokestack Lightnin'," a song built around the image of a moving train, their audiences were familiar with the longing and imagery expressed in the songs. Oftentimes, listeners felt a shared sense of community when they heard the music; they had watched the same trains pass through the country towards new opportunities in the North. African Americans who migrated often reflected back on the places from which they had come, and the Blues served as a link between their old homes and their new urban lives. When Phil and Leonard Chess, two Polish immigrants living in Chicago, began to search for artists to record on their Chess record label in the late 1940s, they decided to focus on Blues artists whose music appealed to the emerging urban African-American community. Through the 1950s and 1960s, Chess recorded artists including Muddy Waters, Howlin' Wolf, and Willie Dixon, in addition to Blues-influenced artists such as Chuck Berry and Bo Diddley, who crossed over into Pop. Like Muddy Waters, most of these musicians had migrated from the South. The repercussions of the Great Migration are far-reaching. Today, much of the restlessness and struggle that the Blues helped to articulate in the Migration era remains central in other forms of American music, including Hip Hop.

After presenting the information above, have learners read "Got a Right to Sing the Blues" by Muddy Waters: Microsoft Word - Handout 1 - Got a Right to Sing the Blues.docx (teachrock.wpenginepowered.com)

Then have learners respond to the following:

- Where did Muddy Waters grow up? What was his name before he became known as Muddy Waters?
- Muddy Waters writes: "*Somebody once asked me what my blues meant. I answered him in one word — 'trouble.'*" Describe what you think he means.
- If your family has ever moved, for what reasons did you move? If you have never moved, what are some reasons people move today? How does it feel to move?

Explain to learners that the class will follow Muddy Waters on his journey north from Mississippi to Chicago, examining how the Blues served as a way for African Americans not just to entertain themselves, but to process their experiences and connect during a period of mass displacement.

In his 1955 article "I Got a Right to Sing the Blues," Muddy Waters says that when he first started playing in Chicago, people called his songs "sharecropper music."

Have learners address the following:

- How did the sharecropping economy in the southern United States function, and how did the system keep sharecroppers stuck in a cycle of poverty?

Distribute the following handout: Microsoft Word - Handout 2 - Blues Lyrics.doc (teachrock.wpenginepowered.com)

Direct learners to Muddy Waters' "Burr Clover Farms." Explain that Muddy recorded this song in 1941, when he was living on a Mississippi farm and working as a sharecropper. Muddy was recorded by Alan Lomax and John Work, two musicologists working for Fisk University and the Library of Congress to study the folk traditions in rural communities. Muddy Waters left the farm and moved to Chicago in 1943, two years after recording this song.

Play audio clip of "Burr Clover Farm Blues" (1941): Burr Clover Farm Blues - TeachRock

Have learners respond to the following:

- According to the lyrics, what seem to be the singer's feelings about the possibility of leaving the farm? How do the lyrics convey the singer's sense of "displacement"?

- Why might some audiences have identified this sound as "sharecropper music"? How do you visualize the setting for a song such as "Burr Clover Farm Blues"?

Distribute "Letter to *Chicago Defender*: Microsoft Word - Handout 3 - Letter to the Chicago Defender.doc (teachrock.wpenginepowered.com)

Have learners read the document and then respond to the following:

- How did the *Defender* reach African Americans who didn't live in Chicago?
- What kind of content did the *Defender* publish to persuade African Americans to leave the South?
- How might northern business owners have benefited from having the *Defender* distributed throughout the South?
- How does the author of the letter describe his life in Lutcher, Louisiana in 1917? What is he trying to achieve by writing to the *Defender*?
- Why does the author ask for the newspaper not to publish his letter?
- The distance between Lutcher in southern Louisiana and Chicago is over 900 miles. What mode of transportation might have been ideal for such a long trip if you did not own a car?

Day 3

Play video clip of Howlin' Wolf performing "Smokestack Lightnin'" (1964): Smokestack Lightnin' - TeachRock

To help make sense of the lyrical imagery, read to learners the following quote attributed to Howlin' Wolf: "We used to sit out in the country and see the trains go by, watch the sparks come out of the smokestack. That was smokestack lightning." Then have learners respond to the following:

- Why might someone living "out in the country" be captivated by the image of a train? Why do you think a train is such a potent symbol in Blues music?
- Why do you think "Smokestack Lightnin'" encapsulated feelings relating to the Great Migration so effectively? How does the song connect to the idea of "displacement"?
- How might you connect the lyrics of "Burr Clover Farm Blues" to "Smokestack Lightnin'"? What story might these two songs tell us when looked at together?

Explain to learners that like Muddy Waters, Howlin' Wolf was born in Mississippi. He later migrated to Chicago, where he recorded "Smokestack Lightnin'" for Chess Records, a company with a focus on recording Blues musicians including Muddy Waters and others.

Distribute the "Chess Records" handout: Microsoft Word - Handout 4 - Chess Records.doc (teachrock.wpenginepowered.com)

Then have learners address the following:

- What did Phil and Leonard Chess observe about the changing demographics of Chicago? How did this influence the music they chose to record?
- How did the Blues music recorded at Chess sound different from earlier Country Blues recordings? Why did the Chess brothers want their recordings to be loud?

- How might the music recorded at Chess have fostered a sense of community for African Americans who had relocated from the South?

Play video clip of "Got My Mojo Working" (1963): Got My Mojo Working - TeachRock

Ask learners to respond to the following:

- How has the sound of Muddy Waters's music changed since his 1941 recording of "Burr Clover Farm Blues"? (*Possible answers include: the inclusion of amplified electric instruments, a full band playing, and faster rhythms.*)
- Think back to Muddy Waters's statement from "Got a Right to Sing the Blues": "Somebody once asked me what my blues meant. I answered him in one word — 'trouble.'" Have learners respond to the following:
- What kinds of "trouble" do you think African Americans might have encountered living and working in large urban centers like Chicago? Why do you think the Blues continued to resonate in African-American communities?

Distribute to each group "African-American Life in the North" handout: Microsoft Word - Handout 5 - African-American Life In The North.doc (teachrock.wpenginepowered.com)

Instruct learners to analyze the materials in the handout to gain a sense of what living quarters, employment opportunities, and community activities were like for African Americans who had moved to the North during the Great Migration era. Each learner will compose one letter in the imagined voice of an African American who has moved to the North and is writing to a relative back in the South. Learners should reference details from their handout to illustrate what their life is like in a northern city. Learners should be sure to answer the following questions:

- What state are you originally from?
- Where do you currently work, and how does it compare to the work you did before moving?
- How would you describe your living situation? How do you spend your time when you are not at work?
- How has your new life in the North met the expectations you had before moving? How has it not?
- What role has Blues music played in your life since moving from the South?
- Where, when, and how do you most often listen to Blues music?

Each learner must also explain what evidence from the handout they chose to highlight in their letter. The project manager is advised to review the rubric that will be used to evaluate the learner.

Day 4

Have learners craft and revise the assignment introduced on Day 4. This assignment must be submitted to the Google Class stream by 11:59 pm tonight.

Day 5

Learners are to provide at least one peer review according to the following criteria:

Rubric-1

The peer reviewed here submitted their assignment to the Google Class stream by 11:59 pm of Day 4. **(0-20 points)**

The assignment submitted included a letter written in the imagined voice of an African American who moved to the North. **(0-10 points)**

The letter is addressed to relative back in the South. **(0-10 points)**

The letter references details from the handout to illustrate what their life is like in a northern city. **(0-10 points)**

The peer reviewed here mentioned what state they are originally from. **(0-10 points)**

The peer reviewed mentioned where they work, and described how it compares to the work the peer reviewed did before moving. **(0-10 points)**

The peer reviewed described their living situation in detail. **(0-10 points)**

The peer reviewed explained how they spend their time when not at work. **(0-10 points)**

The peer reviewed explained how their new life in the North met the expectations they had before moving and how it had not met expectations. **(0-20 points)**

The peer reviewed explained what role Blues music has played in their life since moving from the South. **(0-10 points)**

The peer reviewed explained where, when, and how they most often listen to Blues music. **(0-10 points)**

The peer reviewed explained what evidence from the handout they chose to highlight in their letter. **(0-10 points)**

Total score _____

Day 6

Have learners read "Obama's Secet Weapon in the South": Obama's Secret Weapon In The South: Small, Dead, But Still Kickin' : Krulwich Wonders... : NPR

Then have learners address the following question:

- How did the Country Blues reflect the challenges of sharecropping, racial injustice, and rural poverty in early 20th-century African-American life? Learners need to be sure to make specific references to the artifacts seen and heard in this project.

Have learners read Cliff White's "…Howlin' For The Wolf" (1976): ...Howlin' for the Wolf - TeachRock

After reading, learners are to refer back to Muddy Waters "Got a Right to Sing the Blues": Microsoft Word - Handout 1 - Got a Right to Sing the Blues.docx (teachrock.wpenginepowered.com)

In a written response supplemented by original research, learners are to address the similarities and differences between the experiences and careers of Howlin' Wolf and Muddy Waters. Learners are to consider Howlin' Wolf and Muddy Waters' upbringings, their respective recording careers, their individual migrations northward, and how their music and performance styles compare and contrast. Learners should cite relevant excerpts and quotes from these two texts and reference specific songs by each artist to support their argument.

- Provide the following thesis statement to learners: Country Blues reflected the challenges of sharecropping, racial injustice, and rural poverty in early 20th-century African-American life.
- Provide the structure of the essay: Thesis/into paragraph that establishes structure of the paper:

    Provide also the structure of the paper in terms of supporting paragraphs:

- Country Blues reflected the challenges of sharecropping in early 20th-century African-American life.
- Country Blues reflected the challenges racial injustice in early 20th-century African-American life.
- Country Blues reflected the challenges of rural poverty in early 20th-century African-American life.
- The conclusion: restate the thesis and highlight main points used to support thesis.

Day 7

Review the rubric with learners at the end of Day 6 and start of Day 7 in order to establish as much clarity as possible. Remind learners of the structure expected of their paper (see Day 6). Then introduce learners to RADAR revision method. Provide the class the period to flesh out and revise the writing assignment they began on Day 7. Have learners solicit feedback on their assignment from classmates.

Day 8

Have learners conclude the writing assignment comparing and contrasting the lives of Howlin' Wolf and Muddy Waters. The writing assignment is to be posted to the Google Class stream by 11:59 pm tonight.

Day 9

Learners are to provide at least one peer review according to the following criteria:

Rubric-2

The peer reviewed here submitted their assignment to the Google Class stream by 11:59 pm of Day 8. **(0-20 points)**

The peer reviewed had a thesis statement that was as follows: Country Blues reflected the challenges of sharecropping, racial injustice, and rural poverty in early 20th-century African-American life.

The peer reviewed elaborated the structure of the paper to follow in the opening paragraph: **(0-10 points)**

The first supporting paragraph of the essay delved into Country Blues reflected the challenges of sharecropping in early 20th-century African-American life and used specific details from sources covered during the course of this project. **(0-20 points)**

The second supporting paragraph of the essay delved into Country Blues reflected the challenges racial injustice in early 20th-century African-American life and used specific details from sources covered during the course of this project. **(0-20 points)**

The third supporting paragraph of the essay delved into Country Blues reflected the challenges of rural poverty in early 20th-century African-American life and used specific details from sources covered during the course of this project. **(0-10 points)**

The conclusion of the essay restated the thesis and highlighted main points used to support thesis. **(0-10 points)**

The peer's essay made specific references to the artifacts seen and heard in this project. **(0-20 points)**

Total score _____

Project 6

"The Invention of the American Teenager"

Overview: Learners will investigate how teenagers became a distinct demographic group with its own identity in the postwar years, and, in turn, how their influence helped push Rock and Roll into the mainstream. In so doing, these "boomers" helped secure Rock and Roll's place as the most important popular music of the 20th century.

Objectives: Upon competition of the project, learners will know the growth of teen purchasing power in the 1950s. Learners will know Learners will know the growing financial independence of teenagers, who could now spend their money as individuals without familial obligation. Learners will know the ways American business marketed goods to the new teenage demographic. Learners will know the effects of growing teen independence on the American family in the postwar era. Learners will know the growing influence of teenagers on popular taste and culture. Learners will know the influence of Chuck Berry and others on the representation of teenage life. Learners will also be able to relate popular music to the social context in which it was produced. Learners will also be able to characterize social, economic, and cultural change over time.

Essential Question: How did teenagers become a distinct demographic group in the 1950s?

Grade: High School and University

Subject: History, Social Studies, ELA, General Music

Estimated Time: 5 class sessions (45 – 50-minute classes)

Day 1

The project manager is advised to begin by apprising learners of the following:

In the early 20th century, the period between childhood and adulthood was simply called adolescence, a passing phase between the two main periods in one's life. But in the postwar period, this age cohort – now known as *teenagers* – developed a distinct identity and established itself as an important demographic group that would come to have enormous influence on American life. Because of the postwar economic boom, many white, middle-class teenagers had more leisure time and more spending power than previous generations of young people. If they held jobs, they were increasingly able to keep their earnings rather than contribute them to the support of the family, as they generally did in early generations. American business soon realized the enormous potential of this emerging market, gearing advertising of everything from soda pop to cars in order to cash in on teens' growing purchasing power. Companies in every segment of the entertainment world — records, radio, television, movies – also pursued the new commodified genre of consumer.

After presenting the information above to learners, present any rubrics that will be used to evaluate their performance during the course of the project. Then ask learners to respond to the following:

- Have teenagers always existed?
- How would you characterize the relationship between teenagers and adults?

Display for learners the song lyrics to Chuck Berry' "School Days," which can be located via search engine. Then play the first 1:30 of "School Days" (1957): School Days - TeachRock

Have learners respond to the following:

- Who is the "you" in the song?
- What happens to the person in the song?
- What audience do you imagine Chuck Berry had in mind when he recorded this song in 1957? Who did he think might buy the record?
- What conclusions can you draw from this song about the influence of teenagers on popular music in the 1950s?

Then explain to learners that they will be seeing a series of images depicting teenagers before World War II and then teens in the 1950s. Instruct learners to write down their observations for the first handout: Microsoft Word - Rock Into Pop Handout 1.edited.doc (teachrock.wpenginepowered.com)

Next, show a comparison photograph of a factory girl, aged 14 or 15, taken by photographer Lewis Hine in 1914: AdriennePagnette1911.jpg (640×470) (teachrock.wpenginepowered.com)

Show also the second image, which is of teens in Boston in the late-1940s: 50sPingPongTeens.jpg (661×506) (teachrock.wpenginepowered.com)

Discuss with learners:

- How old are the people in the pictures?
- What is the girl in the first picture doing?
- What are the boys and girls in the second picture doing?
- What do you imagine the girl in the first picture does with the money she earns? Does she keep it for herself, or use it to help support her family?
- Do you think the boys and girls in the second picture have jobs? Why or why not? What kinds of jobs might they have?
- If they do have jobs, what do you think they do with the money they earn? Do they keep it for themselves, or use it to help support their families?
- What do these images suggest about how much leisure time middle-class teenagers had in the postwar years, compared to earlier times? About how much spending money they had?

Inform learners that in 1946 the average weekly income of a teenage boy (allowance plus job earnings) was $2.41. In 1956 the average weekly income of a teenage boy (allowance plus job earnings) was $8.96 (*Time m*agazine, "Bobby-Soxers' Gallup," Aug. 13, 1956).

Ask learners:

- What kinds of things do you imagine the teenager in 1956 would have spent this money on?
- If teenagers in this era were able to spend more money on themselves than teens in earlier times, how do you think this might have affected their relationship with their parents?

Show learners a Coca-Cola ad circa 1940: CocaColaAd1940.jpg (502×652) (teachrock.wpenginepowered.com)

Show learners a 7-Up ad circa 1954: 7up1964.jpg (480×640) (teachrock.wpenginepowered.com)

Compel learners to respond to the following:

- Who do you see in the first advertisement?
- What does the picture in the first advertisement suggest about the relationship between parents and children?
- Who do you see in the second advertisement? Who is no longer in the picture? What does this suggest to you about changes in family life in the 1950s?
- In the first advertisement, whom is Coca-Cola trying to convince to buy its product?
- Who is 7-Up trying to convince to buy its product in the second advertisement?
- Why do you think the advertisers changed their focus in this way between 1940 and 1954?

Then show learners a radio ad from 1938: 38rcavictor2.jpg (400×534) (teachrock.wpenginepowered.com)

And show them a radio ad from 1959: MotorolaAd1959.jpg (503×654) (teachrock.wpenginepowered.com)

Ask learners:

- What is the first advertisement trying to get consumers to buy? Who is most likely going to make the decision about whether to buy it?
- What is the second advertisement trying to get consumers to buy? Who is most likely going to make the decision about whether to buy it?
- Look at the radio in the first advertisement. In what room in the house would it have likely been? Who do you think would have decided what programs to listen to?
- Look at the radio in the second advertisement. How is it different from the radio in the first ad? Where would someone be most likely to use it? Who would have decided what to play on it?
- What conclusions can you draw about how the relationship between teens and their parents changed from the 1930s to the 1950s?
- What conclusions can you draw about how teenagers might have influenced the kinds of music that was played on the radio in 1959?

Day 2

Distribute the following handout to learners (published Aug. 31, 1959): Microsoft Word - Life Magazine Article.edited.doc (teachrock.wpenginepowered.com)

Show the class the following photo from *Life Magazine* illustrating the kinds of goods teens purchased in the 1950s: teengoods.jpg (629×413) (teachrock.wpenginepowered.com)

Provide learners time to read the article distributed and then have them jot down their thoughts and ideas as they pertain to the following questions:

- According to the article, how much money did teenagers spend in a year in 1959?
- General Motors was the largest car manufacturer in the world at the time the article was written. How does the article say teen spending compared to the total sales of GM cars?

- Based on the article, what kinds of things were teens buying in this era? Would you characterize these things as necessities or luxuries?
- Out of that total spending, how much was spent specifically on entertainment? On records?
- If you were a record company executive in 1959, how would this information influence the kinds of artists you signed contracts with and the kinds of songs you asked them to record?

Day 3

Play the final minute of Chuck Berry's "School Days": School Days - TeachRock

Compel learners to respond to the following:

- What does the "you" in the song do after school?
- Does the song suggest that life revolved around the home in this era? What conclusion can you draw from this song about how independent teenagers were in 1957?
- What does the last verse say about Rock and Roll?
- What does the song tell you about who would have been listening to this record?
- What conclusion can you draw from this song about how important Rock and Roll was to the teenage experience in 1957?

Finally, have learners write a short response reflecting on the birth of teen culture in the 1950s. Learners should craft their responses as a narrative from the perspective of the teenage "you" in "School Days," and include details from the readings, photos, and advertisements in their descriptions of teen culture.

Day 4

Have learners reflect on today's marketplace and teen culture and compare it to the teenage demographic of the 1950s. Questions they ought to consider might include:

- On what do teenagers today spend their money? How is that different from what teens spent money on in the 1950s? How is it similar?
- How has technology affected the spending habits of teens since the 1950s?
- How do teens' tastes today influence their households' consumption?
- How does today's music industry attract teen buyers?
- How do other businesses use music to attract teenage customers?
- Overall, do you think teens have less, more, or the same influence over popular culture as they did in the 1950s?

Next, learners are tasked with investigating the relatively new marketing demographic of "tweens" and compare its influence on popular culture both to the that of teenagers today and that of teenagers in the 1950s. Learners are advised to focus on the ways music, fashion, entertainment, and other products have been marketed to all three groups. How are products marketed differently to tweens than to teens?

This response from Day 3 and Day 4 must be posted to the Google Class stream by 11:59 pm tonight.

Day 5

Rubric

Learners will provide at least one peer review according to the following criteria:

The peer reviewed here posted their assignment to the Google Class stream by 11:59 pm of Day 4. **(0-20 points)**

The peer reviewed here wrote a short response reflecting on the birth of teen culture in the 1950s. **(0-20 points)**

In that short response, the peer reviewed crafted their response as a narrative from the perspective of the teenage "you" in "School Days." **(0-20 points)**

In that short response, the peer reviewed included details from the readings, photos, and advertisements in their descriptions of teen culture. **(0-20 points)**

The peer reviewed here delved into the ways music, fashion, entertainment, and other products marketed differently to tweens than to teens. **(0-20 points)**

The peer reviewed here addressed the questions:

On what do teenagers today spend their money? **(0-10 points)**

How is that different from what teens spent money on in the 1950s? **(0-10 points)**

How is it similar? **(0-10 points)**

How has technology affected the spending habits of teens since the 1950s? **(0-10 points)**

How do teens' tastes today influence their households' consumption? **(0-10 points)**

How does today's music industry attract teen buyers? **(0-10 points)**

How do other businesses use music to attract teenage customers? **(0-10 points)**

Overall, do you think teens have less, more, or the same influence over popular culture as they did in the 1950s? **(0-10 points)**

Total score _____

Project 7

"Car Culture in Postwar America"

Overview: Using a selection of songs, statistics, television spots, archival films, and magazine advertisements, learners investigate how the postwar resurgence of the U.S. automotive industry coincided with the rise of the teenager, the two intersecting in Rock and Roll culture.

Objectives: By the end of the project learners will know the role of the Ford Motor Company in establishing private automobile ownership as an essential component of the American experience. Learners will know how the resurgence of automobile manufacturing after WWII coincided with the rise of teen culture. Learners will know the impact of the Interstate Highway Act of 1956 on life in postwar America. Learners will know how Rock and Roll acts including Chuck Berry and the Beach Boys brought together teenage interests in cars and Rock and Roll. Learners will be able to interpret a variety of archival magazine advertisements produced by the Ford Motor Company and General Motors between 1903-1950. Learners will also be able to discuss figurative and connotative meanings of Rock and Roll song lyrics portraying the confluence of teen and auto culture in the United States.

Essential Question: How did car culture intersect with and inspire Rock and Roll?

Grade: High School and University

Subject: History, Social Studies, ELA, General Music

Estimated Time: 5 class sessions (45 – 50-minute classes)

Day 1

The project manager is advised to begin the project by presenting the following information to the class:

In 1949, General Motors introduced the Oldsmobile 88. Dubbed "Futuramic" and advertised as "the lowest-priced car with a 'rocket' engine," the sleek new vehicle epitomized an American fascination with speed, exploration, and space travel in the early 1950s. The Oldsmobile's appeal was so widespread, that in 1951, Jackie Brenston and His Delta Cats (an alternate name for Ike Turner's Kings of Rhythm, with whom Brenston played saxophone and occasionally sang) recorded the song "Rocket 88" — an ode to the fantasy of driving the stylish car. Many historians would argue that "Rocket 88" was the first Rock and Roll song, citing the tremendous raw energy the band brought to the music. Without question, it signaled a connection between car culture and Rock and Roll. Cars had been part of the American experience since the early twentieth century. In 1908, Henry Ford debuted his assembly-line produced Model T. The car's relatively low price and interchangeable parts enabled many middle- and working-class Americans to own, and maintain, a car for the first time. The auto industry boomed through the 1920s, but with the onset of the Great Depression, sales began a sharp decline. In early 1942, America's entry into World War II necessitated a complete halt in the production of domestic passenger vehicles while auto factories were reconfigured for wartime contracts. With no new models available for the duration of the war, car culture was effectively on hiatus. After the Allied powers achieved victory in both the Pacific and European theaters, Americans were filled with a sense of confidence, optimism, and national pride at levels they had never before experienced. Additionally, because the battles of WWII had not been fought on American soil, the U.S. was in a unique position not to *rebuild* from the destruction caused by the war, but rather to *expand*. As soldiers returned home and began to buy houses and start families, suburban communities developed around cities, necessitating not only new roads, but an abundance of brand-new cars to drive those roads. By the time civilian auto production resumed in 1946, many Americans had not owned a new car since before the Depression — if they had ever owned a car at all. With the postwar economy surging, car sales in the United States skyrocketed. The creation of an interstate highway system in 1956 further transformed where people lived, how they got around, who they socialized with, and how they spent their money. A rising population of teenagers, born after the war into a country enjoying an unprecedented surge of prosperity, soon forged an intense and energetic relationship with cars as they became old enough to receive their driver's permits. By the early 1960s, the intersection of car culture and Rock and Roll was well-established and vibrant. Transistor radios became a standard feature on many new car models, allowing increasing numbers of Americans to listen to music while on the road. Songs including Chuck Berry's "No Money Down," Jan & Dean's "Surf City," and the Beach Boys' "Fun, Fun, Fun" emphasized the extent to which the automobile had captured the nation's imagination. The very act of driving had come to symbolize a new-found freedom of movement, particularly for American teenagers.

After presenting the information above to learners, present any rubrics that will be used to evaluate their performance during the course of the project. Then play for the class "Your Permit to Drive" (1951): Your Permit to Drive - General Motors Photographic - TeachRock

Learners are advised to take notes on any phrases the narrator uses to illustrate the societal effects of highways, cars, and driving. Ask learners:

- Why does the narrator refer to a driver's permit as a "round-trip travel ticket," a "passport to pleasure," and a "magic carpet"?
- How might having a car give daily life "new meaning" for millions of people? For a teenager?

Display for learners a photograph from a 1959 issue of *Life Magazine* illustrating the kinds of goods teens purchased in the 1950s. Explain that during the postwar years (approximately 1945-1968), teenagers became a distinct demographic, with many middle-class teens enjoying more leisure time, mobility, and more spending power than previous generations of young people. Ask the class to identify any recognizable items in the photograph, making sure that they notice the two cars near the back of the image. Then as a class, create a list of ways that having access to a car might affect a suburban teenager's lifestyle. List suggestions on the board.

Distribute to learners "Car Culture in Rock and Roll Lyrics": Microsoft Word - Handout 1 - Car Song Lyric Excerpts.docx (teachrock.wpenginepowered.com)

Then play an audio clip of Chuck Berry performing "No Money Down" (1955): No Money Down - TeachRock

Then explain to the class that Chuck Berry is considered one of the founding fathers of Rock and Roll music and that many of his songs present teenage themes and life experiences, such as school, dancing to popular music, and driving. Ask learners:

- How does this song convey a sense of excitement about buying a new car?
- How do the lyrics convey a sense of youth?

Explain to learners that the class is going to explore how cars became a commodity in the lives of millions of Americans, beginning in the early twentieth century. For reference, $850 in 1904 is equal to about $25,000 in 2024.

Display the following Ford Auto ads from 1903 and 1904: Early_Ford_Advertisements.png (1232×581) (teachrock.wpenginepowered.com)

Then have learners respond to the following:

- What phrases stand out in these two advertisements?
- What do these phrases suggest about the segment of the population who could afford a car around 1904?

Explain to learners that cars began to appear in the U.S. during the late-nineteenth and early twentieth centuries. Because they could only be built by hand, one at a time, by highly skilled mechanics, cars were considered a luxury item, reserved only for the wealthiest Americans.

Display for learners 1925 ads for Ford Model T: Ford_Advertisements_1925.png (1436×617) (teachrock.wpenginepowered.com)

Explain to learners that in 1908, the Ford Motor Company revolutionized the automotive industry by introducing the Model T. Ask learners:

- What phrases stand out in these three advertisements? (*Answers should include: "You Can Own This Car Today," "Have Fun with a Ford," "Drive as You Pay," and "Within means of millions."*)
- What are the people in these ads doing? How do the ads target middle- and working-class Americans?
- How has the affordability of a car changed since the ads from 1903 and 1904? How might offering a payment plan allow more people to buy cars?

Day 2

Distribute a handout delving into the nascent days of car culture: Microsoft Word - Handout 2 - Early Car Culture.doc (teachrock.wpenginepowered.com)

Read aloud as a class, then compel learners to respond to the following:

- How were cars constructed *before* Henry Ford's introduction of the assembly line? How did the assembly line help facilitate the beginning of a "car culture" in the United States?
- How were automobile production and sales affected by the Great Depression and America's entry into World War II?
- Why was it important for Americans to make a decision between either making cars for civilian use or making tanks for the U.S. military during World War II? How might wartime rationing of manufactured goods have helped build a sense of national unity?
- How did automobile production and sales change once again after the end of the war? What factors accounted for this change?
- Explain that one of the first new cars to come on the market after World War II was the Oldsmobile 88, a model introduced by General Motors in 1949.

Display that ad for the class: Oldsmobile_88_Ad.jpg (985×1247) (teachrock.wpenginepowered.com)

Play for learners an audio clip of Jackie Brenston and his Delta Cats (1951): <u>Rocket 88 - TeachRock</u>

Learners should use the lyrics in the handout as a guide and pay attention to the ad for the Oldsmobile 88 seen in the clip. Explain that "Rocket 88" went to No. 1 on the *Billboard* Rhythm and Blues chart and is sometimes referred to as the first Rock and Roll song. Then compel learners to respond to the following:

- "How would you describe the rhythm of this song? How would you describe the mood of the vocals?
- How does the magazine ad for the Oldsmobile 88 portray a sense of optimism and progress as it relates to auto culture?
- Why do you think Americans insisted on having the opportunity to travel for pleasure and enjoy leisure time in the years following a depression and a war?

Play the Oldsmobile "88" television commercial (1953): <u>Television Commercial for the Oldsmobile "88" - TeachRock</u>

Explain to learners that Mel Torme was a Pop singer with a career that began in the 1930s. After WWII, many companies began to feature celebrities in their advertising campaigns, which was a new and novel idea back then. While the music of Mel Torme helped to sell cars to adults, the teen audience of the 1950s was often looking for something more beat-driven and raw. Have learners respond to the following:

- How are the rhythm and vocals of this commercial jingle different from the rhythm and vocals of "Rocket 88" by Jackie Brenston and His Delta Cats?
- Between the commercial jingle and "Rocket 88", which song do you think appealed more to the tastes of teenagers? Why?

Day 3

Explain to the class that car culture wouldn't have had the effects it did if it didn't also have the infrastructure to cultivate changing driving behaviors in the United States. Then distribute to learners a handout delving into The Interstate Highway Act and Car Production statistics: <u>Microsoft Word - Handout 3 - Car Ownership Statistics.doc (teachrock.wpenginepowered.com)</u>

Read the document as a class and then compel the learners to respond to the following:

- How did the passage of the Highway Act of 1956 incentivize Americans to buy cars?

Graph-A Questions

- What happens to the population of Americans aged 15-19 years just after the passage of the Highway Act in 1956?
- Why do you think this population segment changes so drastically at this particular time?

Graph-B Questions

- How do the rates of homeownership and car ownership change around the start of the Great Depression in 1929?

- How does the rate of car ownership change once the United States enters WWII at the end of 1941?
- Why does the rate of car ownership decrease when the U.S. enters the war?
- What happens to the rates of homeownership and car-owning households between 1945 and 1965?
- Which rate increases more?
- What conclusions can we make about the relationship between homeownership and car ownership after approximately 1950?
- When a parent purchases a second car, who do you think is often times the recipient of the older car?

Next, display a Ford magazine ad circa 1950: 1950_Ford_Ad_Two_Car_Garage.jpg (477×635) (teachrock.wpenginepowered.com)

Have learners respond to the following:

- What phrase stands out in this advertisement?
- What is the phrase referring to?
- How does this ad relate to the graphs we just looked at?
- What age do the "children" in this ad appear to be? What is the family depicted in this advertisement doing? (The project manager is advised to read to the class that the teenagers are saying, "Don't worry, Mom. If Pop isn't back in time, we can take everything in the Country Squire.")
- How has Ford's messaging changed since the ads we examined from before World War II?

Day 4

Play for learners The Beach Boys performing "Fun, Fu, Fun": Fun, Fun, Fun - TeachRock

Explain to learners that they will research a driving-related song of their choice and write a short essay discussing how the song relates to and expands upon the materials discussed in class, if and how it references any specific car models or driving-related social activities (if applicable), as well how the song illustrates the teenage *idea* of having a car. Learners may select a song from the following list or choose another song with the project manager's approval:

- The Beach Boys – "Don't Worry Baby"
- The Beach Boys – "Little Deuce Coupe"
- The Beatles – "Drive My Car"
- Bruce Springsteen – "Thunder Road"
- Bruce Springsteen – "Used Cars"
- Charlie Ryan – "Hot Rod Lincoln"
- Chuck Berry – "No Particular Place to Go"
- The Clash – "Brand New Cadillac"
- Coolio – "Fantastic Voyage"
- Gary Numan – "Cars"
- The Hondells – "Little Honda"
- J. Frank Wilson and the Cavaliers – "Last Kiss"
- Jan & Dean – "Dead Man's Curve"
- Jan & Dean – "Surf City"

- Johnny Cash – "One Piece at a Time"
- Kanye West – "Drive Slow"
- Neil Young with Stephen Stills – "Long May You Run"
- Prince – "Little Red Corvette"
- Queen – "I'm in Love With My Car"
- Ronny and the Daytonas – "G.T.O."
- The Rip Chords – "Hey Little Cobra"
- The Shangri-Las – "Give Us Your Blessings"
- The Surfer Girls – "Draggin' Wagon"
- Tracy Chapman – "Fast Car"
- The Trashmen – "A-Bone"
- War – "Low Rider"
- Wilson Pickett – Mustang Sally"

The essay is due at 11:59 pm tonight.

Day 5

Learners will provide at least two peer reviews according to the following criteria:

Rubric

The peer reviewed here submitted their assignment to the Google Class stream by 11:59 pm of Day 4. **(0-20 points)**

The essay submitted specifically addressed how the song relates to and expands upon the materials discussed in class. **(0-10 points)**

The essay submitted references a specific car models and/or driving-related social activities. **(0-10 points)**

The essay contextualizes the teenage idea/fetish of having a car and what having a car symbolizes to the American teen. **(0-10 points)**

The essay submitted was free of spelling and grammar errors. **(0-10 points)**

Total score _____

Project 8

"Rock and Roll Goes to the Movies"

Overview: Learners assume the role of entertainment industry professionals responsible for marketing a selection of movies from the early Rock and Roll era. Following an examination of trailers, posters, newspaper articles, and the Motion Picture Production Code of 1930, learners will present to the class on the various stakeholders that helped shape the way Rock and Roll culture was introduced to mainstream movie audiences in the 1950s.

Objectives: Upon completion of this lesson, learners will know the various subgenres of Rock and Roll movies that appeared in the mid-to-late 1950s. Learners will know the Anxieties surrounding the release and popularity of the film *Blackboard Jungle* due to its depictions of race and juvenile delinquency. Learners will know how the Production Code was used to monitor film content prior to the 1968 adoption of a ratings system. Learners will know the specialized roles of various professional organizations in producing, marketing, and exhibiting American movies. Learners will be able to analyze historical documents, periodicals, and film trailers. Learners will be able to make connections between a selection of films concerning Rock and Roll culture and concerns over the perceived threat of juvenile delinquency.

Essential Question: How did movies help to introduce Rock and Roll culture to mainstream American audiences in the 1950s?

Grade: High School and University

Subject: History, Social Studies, ELA, General Music

Estimated Time: 5 class sessions (45 – 50-minute classes)

Day 1

The project manager is advised to apprise learners of the following:

As the influence of teenagers expanded in the 1950s, it did not take long for movie studios to tap into their fascination with Rock and Roll. Some historians argue that the first so-called "Rock and Roll movie" to cause a sensation was *Blackboard Jungle* (1955), a film depicting the struggles of a high school teacher with a class full of "juvenile delinquents." The film opened to the sound of "Rock Around the Clock" by Bill Haley & His Comets. The song was reportedly played at such a high volume that teenage audiences rose from their seats to either dance in the aisles or to vandalize the auditorium, depending on the media coverage. *Blackboard Jungle* sent "Rock Around the Clock" directly to the top of the Billboard charts, while the movie's notoriety led to widespread censorship. The controversy only further increased public interest in Rock and Roll, and Hollywood was ready to meet the demand. In the aftermath of *Blackboard Jungle*, many other films emerged that featured Rock and Roll culture and its world. Among these were musical films such as *Rock Around the Clock*—light on storyline and constructed mainly as a showcase for the top performers of the day. There were also films in which the singing star *became* the movie star, typified by the films of Elvis Presley. Movies including *Jailhouse Rock* drew large audiences who came to see Elvis sing his hits while playing dramatic—but always musical—leading men. And then there were films that did not feature popular music at all, but nonetheless managed to capture the Rock and Roll attitude—particularly when they told stories of teenage life from the perspective of the teens themselves. In *Rebel Without a Cause*, James Dean did not sing a note, but captured the internal struggles of adolescent angst on film as no one had before. Dean's rebellious screen persona would become as emblematic as Elvis' swiveling hips in defining the look of early Rock and Roll.

After presenting the info above, along with any rubrics that might be used to evaluate learners during the course of the project, play the trailer for *Blackboard Jungle* (1955): Blackboard Jungle - Trailer 2b (youtube.com)

Play the trailer for *Rebel Without a Cause* (1955): Rebel Without a Cause - Trailer - YouTube

Play the trailer for *Rock Around the Clock* (1956): Rock Around the Clock Trailer - TeachRock

Play the trailer for *Jailhouse Rock* (1957): Jailhouse Rock Official Trailer Elvis Presley Movie 1957 HD - YouTube

Learners are expected to take notes on any words and phrases the narrator uses to describe the onscreen action and music. Explain to the class that each of these films addressed concerns about teenagers in the mid-1950s, particularly the perceived threat of juvenile delinquency and the rising influence of Rock and Roll culture.

After the clip, have learners jot down their thoughts and ideas as they pertain to:

- What is this movie about? How does the film depict teenagers?
- By playing "Rock Around the Clock" over the image of "teenage savages," what does the film seem to suggest about Rock and Roll music?
- Explain that *Blackboard Jungle* was the first movie to feature a Rock and Roll song on its soundtrack. After the film's release, "Rock Around the Clock" went to number one on Billboard's Pop charts, where it remained for eight weeks. However, due to some people's concerns over the content of the film, *Blackboard Jungle* was banned in several American cities.

A June 4, 1955 *New York Times* reported the ban on *Blackboard Jungle* in Atlanta. Some of the terms used in the article to justify the banning of the film in Atlanta, Georgia, were "a film with a racial element," and describe the film as "immoral, obscene, licentious."

Compel learners to jot down their thoughts and ideas as they pertain to the following:

- Based on your observations from watching the trailer, do you think the ban was warranted?
- Do you think the controversy over the film helped or hurt the popularity of the song "Rock Around the Clock?" Explain your answer.

Day 2

Divide the class into four groups.

Provide group 1 a handout which can be located at the following web address: Microsoft Word - Handout 1 - The Film Studio.doc (teachrock.wpenginepowered.com)

Provide group 2 a handout which can be located at the following web address: Microsoft Word - Handout 2 - The Record Label.doc (teachrock.wpenginepowered.com)

Provide group 3 a handout which can be located at the following web address: <u>Microsoft Word - Handout 3 - The MPAA.doc (teachrock.wpenginepowered.com)</u>

Provide group 4 a handout which can be located at the following web address: <u>Microsoft Word - Handout 4 - The Theater Owners of America.doc (teachrock.wpenginepowered.com)</u>

Each group will represent a group of 1950s entertainment industry professionals. Each team should review their handout which explains the role of their organization and a set of criteria which the team will use to review the movies. Each team will have a different final report to share with the class. Check for understanding before playing the first trailer.

Play the trailer *Blackboard Jungle* (1955): <u>Blackboard Jungle - Trailer 2b (youtube.com)</u>

Play the trailer for *Rebel Without a Cause* (1955): <u>Rebel Without a Cause - Trailer - YouTube</u>

Play the trailer for *Rock Around the Clock* (1956): <u>Rock Around the Clock Trailer - TeachRock</u>

Play the trailer for *Jailhouse Rock* (1957): <u>Jailhouse Rock Official Trailer Elvis Presley Movie 1957 HD - YouTube</u>

Now that each trailer has been screened, allow teams a few minutes to discuss and reach their final conclusions about the films. Have each team present their findings to the class. For presentations, teams should elect several representatives to introduce their professional organization, explain their assigned task, and describe their methodology to determine which movie to promote or restrict. To check for understanding, each learner will submit to the project manager an "exit ticket." On the paper, learners need to write 3-4 sentences in which they pick one of the four trailers viewed during the project (including *Blackboard Jungle*) and discuss why they would most want to see that movie in its entirety. Learners may base their decision on the film's subject matter, music featured, star actors, the reviews it received upon first release, or any combination of these factors.

Day 3

Introduce learners to proper MLA citation. The Purdue Owl website is an actionable didactic source for this. Then introduce learners to the structure of an argumentative essay:

- Thesis statement establishing which side of the debate the essayist is choosing to support.
- Opening paragraph that elaborates the structure of the essay.
- Supporting paragraph one – sentence in support of thesis followed by evidence from a source provided.
- Supporting paragraph two – sentence in support of thesis followed by evidence from a source provided.
- Supporting paragraph 3 – sentence in support of thesis followed by evidence from a source provided.
- Conclusion – restate thesis and rehash main supporting points.

Distribute an article from the April 9, 1955 issue of *Harrison's Reviews* titled, "Intelligent Handling of a Touchy Problem." The handout can be located at the following web address: <u>Microsoft Word - Handout 5 - Blackboard Jungle Solutions.doc (teachrock.wpenginepowered.com)</u>

Explain that Harrison's Reviews was a motion picture trade journal for independent theater owners that published film reviews and professional advice for theater owners. After learners have read the article, have them outline a 300-word op-ed to *Harrison's Reviews* responding to the RKO Theatre in New Brunswick, New Jersey's decision to run a special trailer at the conclusion of each screening of *Blackboard Jungle*. Have learners specifically address the following questions in their op-ed/argumentative essay:

- Do you agree with the management's decision? If yes, explain why you think the strategy helped the community, and if no, explain what you might have done differently to address people's concerns about the film. Either way, the learner must write an argumentative essay. Learners must also use "Intelligent Handling of a Touchy Problem" to support their argument one way or the other and cite that source in proper MLA citation.

Day 4

Expose learners to the RADAR revision method. Compel learners to write and revise their op-ed, which must be posted by 11:59 pm tonight.

Day 5

Learners will provide at least two peer reviews according to the following criteria:

Rubric

The peer reviewed here submitted their argumentative essay to the Google Class stream by 11:59 pm of Day 4. **(0-20 points)**

The essay began with a clear thesis statement establishing which side of the controversy they are supporting. **(0-10 points)**

The opening paragraph elaborates the structure of the essay. **(0-10 points)**

The first supporting paragraph begins with a sentence in support of thesis and is followed by evidence from the article. **(0-20 points)**

The second supporting paragraph begins with a sentence in support of thesis and is followed by evidence from the article. **(0-20 points)**

The third supporting paragraph begins with a sentence in support of thesis and is followed by evidence from the article. **(0-20 points)**

The conclusion of the essay restates thesis and rehashes main supporting points. **(0-20 points)**

The essay used "Intelligent Handling of a Touchy Problem" as a source. **(0-10 points)**

The essayist properly cited the source used: "Intelligent Handling of a Touchy Problem." **(0-10 points)**

The essayist used knowledge developed during the course of the project in order to present their argument. **(0-10 points)**

The essay was free of spelling and grammar errors. **(0-10 points)**

Total score _____

Project 9

"Rock 'n' Roll and the American Dream"

Overview: In this project, learners will explore the persistence of the American Dream by juxtaposing the writings of Horatio Alger Jr. and John Steinbeck with the artistic output of Elvis Presley and Johnny Cash. If the American Dream as an ideology has always been a balance between myth and reality, these artists, and Rock and Roll culture more generally, gave the myth something real. Through a survey of literature, album art, songs, television news reports, film, and other materials, learners will examine how these artists became symbols of the American Dream for their many fans. Taking Sam Phillips as a case study, this lesson explores the role of the producer in the recording studio as one defined by an ability to guide the recording process but also to affect the wider cultural context. This project looks at the way Sam Phillips' approach in some ways reflects the trend of urbanization in the American South. Like Phillips, many of his artists came from rural backgrounds and were seeking the benefits of urban life. That move toward the urban, and the racial mixing it fostered, seemed encoded in the music. Finally, the lesson looks at Phillip's guidance of a young Elvis Presley and suggests how the music they produced created an opening for African-American music to "crossover" into mainstream American popular music.

Objectives: Learners will know how authors Horatio Alger, Jr. and John Steinbeck interpreted the American Dream in very different ways through their fiction. Learners will know How Elvis Presley and Johnny Cash exemplified elements of the American Dream throughout their successful musical careers. Learners will know how Graceland became a geographical and allegorical symbol for Elvis Presley's rags-to-riches story. Learners will also be able to draw thematic comparisons between the works of Horatio Alger, Jr. and John Steinbeck. Learners will consider the connection between the American Dream and Elvis Presley and Johnny Cash's cultural impact in postwar America. Learners will know about Sam Phillips, his Memphis Recording Service Studio and Sun Records label in Memphis, Tennessee. Learners will know about Elvis Presley's early career and its social significance. Learners will know about the *de facto* racial segregation that often-separated Pop and Rhythm and Blues music in the early and mid-20th century U.S. Learners will know about trends of urbanization in the American South during the early and mid-20th century. Learners will know how race affected an individual's access to opportunity in 1950s American South. Learners will know how Sam Phillips helped produce music that represented a mixing of sounds previously considered "white" or "black." Learners will be able to understand connections between popular culture and the time, place and social circumstances in which it was created. Learners will be able to consider how popular culture can effect social change. Learners will be able to discuss how the careers of particular artists reflect the attitudes of the society from which they emerged. Learners will be able to make connections between popular culture and historical events such as urbanization and segregation. Learners will be able to integrate and evaluate information presented in visual, oral and audio formats.

Essential Questions: What is the American Dream and how did Elvis Presley and Johnny Cash personify its ideals? How did the recordings Sam Phillips produced at Sun Records, including Elvis Presley's early work, reflect trends of urbanization and integration in the 1950s American South?

Grade: High School and University

Subject: Social Studies, History, ELA, General Music

Estimated Time: 10 class sessions (45 – 50-minute classes)

Day 1

The project manager is advised to apprise learners of any rubrics that might be used to evaluate them during the course of the project. Then, display for the class two album covers: Elvis Presley's *50,000,000 Elvis Fans Can't Be Wrong* (1959) and Johnny Cash's *At Folsom Prison* (1968). Have learners respond to the following questions:

- How different do Elvis and Cash dress?
- What is different about their physical poses?
- What's different about their personalities (if apparent)?
- What's different about their album titles and any other visible design elements?
- What assumptions might they make about the artists and their music based on the album covers?

Then have learners write "The American Dream" on their paper. Ask them to spend 5 minutes conceiving and writing down a definition in 1-2 sentences. Have them share definitions aloud.

The project manager is advised to present the following information to the class:

The American Dream—the idea that every person who calls him or herself an American has the opportunity to achieve a better life, to find a voice within the structure of the "nation," to *rise*—is a concept that deeply permeates American identity. The American Dream is an essential part of the national lore used to explain what it means to be a citizen of the United States. The story is everywhere: The well-known biography of Abraham Lincoln begins in a Kentucky log cabin and ends in the White House. Horatio Alger Jr.'s nineteenth-century novels depict characters rising from rags to riches, as achieved through honest work, courage, and perseverance. In the 1930s, novelist John Steinbeck published *Of Mice and Men,* in which the protagonists, migrant laborers George and Lennie, maintain their dream of owning a farm even as they face brutal poverty and economic disenfranchisement. Just as Lincoln, Alger, and Steinbeck offered different views into the concept of the American Dream, Elvis Presley and Johnny Cash participated in updating the story for the Rock and Roll era, rising from working class beginnings to become legends in American life and culture. In the eyes of his fans, Elvis embodies the seductive lore of the American Dream. He was born at home in a two-room house in Tupelo, Mississippi in the midst of the Great Depression. The family later moved to Memphis, where they lived in a series of rented rooms and a public housing project while Elvis attended high school. All members of the Presley family worked several jobs, including Elvis, who worked as a machinist and drove a truck. Even in his earliest interviews, Elvis would say that all he wanted to do was to make enough money to buy his parents a house of their own, reminding his audience of his roots in the working class and how far he'd risen. Elvis pulled himself up by the proverbial bootstraps, so the legend went, by strumming his guitar and grating his hips. By the spring of 1957, barely three years after recording "That's All Right," his first single for Sun Records, Elvis had already become a Pop superstar, both as a musician and a Hollywood actor. It was that year when he purchased Graceland, a mansion in the Memphis suburbs. In the twenty years the Presley family lived in the home, the name "Graceland" became nearly interchangeable with Elvis himself, a symbol of the singer's meteoric rise to fame and the possibility of a real "American Dream" coming true. Upon his death in 1977, Graceland became a spiritual mecca for music fans from all over the world looking to pay homage to the (white) King of Rock and Roll. The American Dream story of Johnny Cash shares some similarities to the Elvis narrative, but with several key differences in the way Cash related to his audience and displayed his arrival. Born in Arkansas three years before Elvis, Cash was one of seven children. He grew up in a federal agricultural resettlement community, part of Franklin Roosevelt's New Deal, where the Cash family lived in a modest house and farmed the surrounding cotton fields. After serving in the U.S. Air Force, Cash worked in a Memphis appliance store. He first auditioned for Sam Phillips at Sun Records in 1954, not long after Elvis recorded his first songs on the same label. While both musicians enjoyed remarkable success, Elvis and Cash ultimately adopted very different public personas. Elvis became a teen idol, releasing pop records and starring in movies, while Cash cultivated an adult-oriented Country audience and wrote songs to suit his self-made "outlaw" image, including "Folsom Prison Blues" and "Don't Take Your Guns to Town." Elvis wore long sideburns and dressed in flamboyant colors and materials. Cash became known as the "Man in Black," a reference to his dark and somber suits, which reflected his desire to memorialize those downtrodden people who had not, for whatever reason, achieved the mythical American Dream. While Elvis established a musical residency in Las Vegas, where several of Elvis' own showbusiness idols had performed, Cash strayed from his busy touring schedule to play free shows for inmates at Folsom and San Quentin State Prisons. The exceptional lives of Elvis Presley and Johnny Cash are pivotal tales that became representations of the American Dream, demonstrating the ability of Rock and Roll culture to transport a person from the margins of society to a place of power, wealth, and universal recognition.

Day 2

Show learners clips of Elvis on the Milton Berle show in 1956: Elvis Presley - Hound Dog - Milton Berle Show - 05 June 1956 (youtube.com)

Show learners clips of Cash on "Ranch Party in 1957: Johnny Cash - I Walk the Line (Ranch Party 1957) in Color - YouTube

Explain that for a young musician in the 1950s, it was considered a major accomplishment to appear on one of these network television shows. Have learners jot down responses to the following:

- What traits do these artists seem to have in common?
- What traits make each of these artists unique?

Distribute to the class: Microsoft Word - HANDOUT 1 - Horatio Alger.docx (teachrock.org)

As a class, read aloud the short biography of Alger and an excerpt from one of his stories. Then have learners jot ideas and thoughts as they pertain to the following:

- What is Dick (the protagonist) likely to achieve by diving off the boat to save the drowning child?
- Based on this scene, what does Alger imply about the protagonist's moral character?
- In a larger scope, what does Alger suggest about a person's opportunity to achieve upward mobility in America? In other words, what traits does an American need in order to succeed?

Distribute to the class: Microsoft Word - HANDOUT 2 - John Steinbeck.docx (teachrock.org)

As a class, read aloud this short biography of Steinbeck and an excerpt from *Of Mice and Men* (1937). Have learners jot thoughts and ideas as they pertain to the following:

- In passage 1, what kind of imagery does George use to describe the farm to Lennie? How does George's vision connect to the idea of the American Dream?
- In passage 2, how does Crooks respond to George and Lennie's dream of owning a farm? What does Crooks' observation suggest about the state of the American Dream during the time of the Great Depression?
- Explain how Steinbeck's understanding of the American Dream is similar to or different from that of Alger's.

Day 3

Distribute to learners the following document: Microsoft Word - HANDOUT 3 - Elvis Houses.docx (teachrock.org)

Have learners respond to the following:

- How big is the house?
- How many rooms might a house like this have?
- How is it decorated?
- What construction materials can you see?
- Who do you think might live in a house like this?

Then have learners describe Graceland using the questions above.

Show the class Elvis' Graceland on the cover of his 1974 live album. Ask learners:

- Why they think the decision was made to put the house on the album cover?
- What statement does this make about Elvis and his relationship to the idea of the American Dream?

Play the "Love Me Tender" movie trailer: Love Me Tender Trailer - TeachRock

Have learners jot down their thoughts and ideas regarding the following:

- What do you notice about Elvis' performance style and the character he is playing on screen?
- Why might a wide, popular audience be attracted to Elvis in this film?
- What are some of the titles you see in the trailer? How do these titles support the real-life story of Elvis' emergence as a superstar?

Distribute "The Man in Black" to learners: Microsoft Word - HANDOUT 4 - The Man in Black V2.docx (teachrock.org)

As a class, review the short biography of Cash detailing his persona as the "Man in Black" and his identification with marginalized people, including Native Americans and prisoners. Then play an audio clip of "Folsom Prison Blues" from Cash's performance at Folsom Prison: "Folsom Prison Blues" - from At Folsom Prison - TeachRock

Explain that while Cash first released the song in 1955, this version is from a live performance for the inmates of Folsom Prison and was recorded in 1968. Have learners jot down their thoughts and ideas as they pertain to the following:

- What kind of imagery does Cash evoke in the song?
- In this recording, Cash is performing before an audience of inmates. However, "Folsom Prison Blues" became one of his most popular and famous songs. Why do you think this song might appeal to a wider audience?
- Does this song seem to align more to Alger or Steinbeck's vision of the American Dream? How?

Day 4

Distribute "The King and I: A Visit to Graceland": Microsoft Word - HANDOUT 5 - A Visit to Graceland.docx (teachrock.wpenginepowered.com)

Have learners read the essays. Then compel them to imagine that they have just visited Graceland as a tourist and write a one-page letter to a friend or family member describing their trip. Have learners be sure to include their own thoughts about what the American Dream means to them personally and how Elvis' life, as displayed at Graceland, compares to their own ideas for a successful life. Be sure learners revise the letter so that it is free of spelling and grammar errors. The letter must be submitted to the Google Class Stream by 11:59 pm tonight.

Day 5

Learners will provide at least one peer review according to the following criteria:

The peer reviewed here submitted their letter to the Google Class by 11:59 pm of Day 4 **(0-20 points)**

The peer reviewed here submitted a polished letter – no spelling or grammar errors. **(0-10 points)**

The peer reviewed here described their trip to Graceland. **(0-10 points)**

The peer reviewed included their own thoughts and ideas about what the American Dream means to them personally. **(0-10 points)**

The peer reviewed wrote about Elvis' life, as displayed at Graceland, and used that emblem as a means of thinking about their own ideas for a successful life. **(0-10 points)**

Day 6

As the U.S. recording industry grew in the first half of the 20th century, so too did the roles of those involved in producing recordings. A "producer" became one or more of many things: talent scout, studio owner, record label owner, repertoire selector, sound engineer, arranger, coach and more. Throughout the 1950s, producer Sam Phillips embodied several of these roles, choosing which artists to record at his Memphis studio and often helping select the material they would play. Phillips released some of the recordings on his Sun Records label, and sold other recordings to labels such as Chess in Chicago. Though Memphis was segregated in the 1950s, Phillips' studio was not. He was enamored with black music and, as he states in "Soundbreaking, Episode One," wished to work specifically with black musicians. Phillips attributed his attitude, which was progressive for the time, to his parents' strong feelings about the need for racial equality and the years he spent working alongside African Americans at a North Alabama farm. Phillips quickly established his studio as a hub of Southern African-American Blues, recording and producing albums for artists such as Howlin' Wolf and B.B. King and releasing what many consider the first ever Rock and Roll single, "Rocket 88" by Jackie Breston and His Delta Cats. But Phillips was aware of the obstacles African-American artists of the 1950's faced; regardless of his enthusiasm for their music, he knew those recordings would likely never "crossover" and be heard or bought by most white listeners. Phillips' assistant Marion Keiske remembers him remarking that if he "could find a white man who had the Negro sound and the Negro feel," he could get the whole country to listen. In 1953 a young man entered Phillip's studio and asked Keiske about purchasing studio time. The singer, Elvis Presley, recorded two ballads for his mother and impressed Keiske enough that she made a note of his name. About a year later, at Keiske's urging, Phillips invited Presley to return to his studio with the intention of having him record a few more ballads. The sessions were initially lackluster and had nearly drawn to a close when Presley and the other two musicians (guitarist Scotty Moore and bassist Bill Black) began goofing around with a version of "That's All Right," a song penned and recorded by African-American musician Arthur Crudup. Phillips liked what he heard and encouraged Presley to do it again, this time for the record. "That's All Right" marked the beginning of a run of hits for Presley, some of which are covers of songs previously recorded by African-American artists. "That's All Right" ultimately helped to launch an era in which styles associated with African-American musicians began moving into "mainstream" American culture.

Play for learners "What Does a Producer Do?": What Does a Producer Do? - TeachRock

Compel learners take notes on the possible roles played by producers. Then have them respond to the following:

- Based on what you just heard, what do you think a producer does?
- In what ways do you think a producer might be important to an artist who is recording an album?
- Can you think of anyone in your life that plays a role similar to that of a "producer"? How might you benefit from that person's assistance?

Play "Sam Phillips and Sun Records": Sam Phillips and Sun Records - TeachRock

Have learners respond to the following:

- How do the speakers characterize Phillips' role at Sun Records? What were his goals?
- How might an artist exemplify the "individualism in the extreme" that Phillips was reportedly seeking? Can you think of any modern artists that might represent "individualism in the extreme"? Why does that matter?
- Why do you think Phillips stressed his intentions to get "black folks" into his studio?

Distribute to learners a handout on Sam Phillips: *Handout 1 - Sam Phillips (teachrock.wpenginepowered.com)

Have learners read the document. Then look at the map and population data on the second page of the handout. Next, have learners jot down their thoughts and ideas as the relate to the following questions:

- What do you notice about the population of Memphis in each decade of the census data shown here?
- Is there anything you see on this map that might have made Memphis an obvious choice or an easy place to relocate to?

Day 7

Inform learners that according to 1950 census data, the population of Memphis was 37% "non-white" (the only census categories at the time were "white" and "non-white") and the majority of that 37% percent was African-American. Much of the transplanted population had arrived in Memphis from rural areas in Mississippi, Alabama, Tennessee and Texas. Explain to learners that both Sam Phillips and many of the black musicians he recorded in the 1950s came to Memphis from rural farming communities in the surrounding states.

Break learners into four groups for the "Gallery Walk of the Rural and Urban South circa 1950" activity. Then distribute the following discussion-question packet, which can be located here: *Handout 2 - Gallery Walk Discussion Questions (teachrock.wpenginepowered.com)

Have each group choose a "scribe" who will record their answers to the questions as they take the Gallery Walk. The project manager is to place each of the following documents at a different wall in the room. The groups are to spend some time at each station examining the document.

Document A:

*Gallery Walk Station 1 - Attire (teachrock.wpenginepowered.com)

Document B:

*Gallery Walk Station 2 - Labor (teachrock.wpenginepowered.com)

Document C:

*Gallery Walk Station 3 - Food (teachrock.wpenginepowered.com)

Document D:

*Gallery Walk Station 4 - Socialization (teachrock.wpenginepowered.com)

Provide the scribe a few moments to finish up and then reconvene the class. After learners have visited the Gallery Walk Stations with their groups, ask them to engage in a conversation based on the following questions:

- What do you think it was about the "urban" that attracted so many young people, both white and black?
- Thinking about the "urban" images you saw in the Gallery Walk, why do you think Marty Stuart characterized the 1950s Memphis as a "black cat's town"?

Explain to the class that Elvis, like Sam Phillips, moved to Memphis and was drawn to black life there at a time when the reach of segregation extended even to the *Billboard* record sales charts. The "Rhythm & Blues" chart represented "black" music separate from the main "Top Singles" charts. There were no songs from 1954 that appear in the top spots of both charts.

Next, play for learners a clip about the crossover success of Phillips and Elvis: Sam Phillips Elvis Presley and Crossover Success - TeachRock

Have learners jot down answers to the following questions:

- What is it that Phillips was so sure Elvis "could do" as an artist? What was Phillips hoping Elvis would accomplish?

- Thinking back to what we've learned about the role of a "producer" in this lesson, how did Phillips "produce" Elvis?
- Why do you think we hear "That's All Right" referred to as a "magic moment" and that through the recording of the song Phillips "freed the soul" of Elvis Presley?
- Based on what you know about Sam Phillips, why was he an ideal producer for the young Elvis Presley?
- Instruct your learners to revisit the images of people they saw in the Gallery Walk on Day ?, then have them jot down their thoughts and ideas to the following questions:
- In what ways could the recording sessions which produced "That's All Right" represent Memphis and urbanization in the South at this time?
- In what ways did Sam Phillips use his position as a music producer to produce a cultural connection that extends far beyond a song?
- In what ways might Sam Phillips' decisions as a producer have had a positive impact on American race politics?

Day 8

Inform learners that Sam Phillips was a proponent of integration and racial equality in the American South at a time when such a position was unpopular or even dangerous. Moreover, he acted on his beliefs, not just recording and producing black artists, but advocating on behalf of their work. Phillips came from a low-income family, lost his father when he was a teenager, and had to support his mother and siblings. Despite the challenges, Phillips finally succeeded. In many ways, Phillips' life and career represent what many have called the "American Dream." Yet, however hard Phillips had to work, he had one constant benefit, especially in the American South during segregation: he was white. Imagine Phillips in a similar position as a young man, but as an African-American young man.

Compel learners to recall the images displayed during the Gallery Walk, the discussions of music and race throughout the project in an effort to address the following questions:

- Phillips took out bank loans to open his recording studio. Do you think a 27-year-old African-American in Memphis have been approved for a business loan in 1950?
- How would a young African-American have gathered or saved the money necessary to open a studio?
- Before opening a studio, Phillips learned about music technology by working at a radio station. Do you think a young black man in 1945 would have had this opportunity?
- Presley used Arthur Crudup's song and elements of African-American performance style to reach a large White audience, what do you think Crudup could have done to reach the same audience? Do you think it would have been possible?
- Finally, provide learners with the following thesis statement: In some ways Sam Phillips, Johnny Cash, and Elvis Pressley are emblematic of the American Dream but in other ways their lives underscore the racial component that was deeply enmeshed in ideas of the American Dream.

Provide learners the remainder of the period to review their notes and work from this project. Their task for the day is to define the American Dream from what was learned earlier in the project. They also need to scan their work for evidence that Elvis, Cash, and Phillips embodied the American Dream. The project manager is advised to remind learners of the criteria in the rubric so they can guide themselves through the process as expediently as possible.

Day 9

Learners are to be reminded of the expectations as outlined in the rubric (see Day 10). Learners are expected to the period to review their notes to conclude crafting the essay begun on Day 8. The structure of the essay should be as follows:

Thesis statement: In some ways Sam Phillips, Johnny Cash, and Elvis Pressley are emblematic of the American Dream but in other ways their lives underscore the racial component that was deeply enmeshed in ideas of the American Dream.

Opening paragraph (after the thesis statement) that establishes the structure of the essay and defines "American Dream" according to the knowledge gained during Days 1 – 4.

Supporting paragraph 1 – begins with a topic sentence that supports the first part of the thesis statement (In some ways Sam Phillips, Johnny Cash, and Elvis Pressley are emblematic of the American Dream). Use evidence learned during the course of the project to support your answer.

Supporting paragraph 2 – begins with a topic sentence that supports the second part of the thesis statement (their lives underscore the racial component that was deeply enmeshed in ideas of the American Dream). Use evidence learned during the course of the project to support your answer.

Conclude the essay by restating the thesis and highlighting some of the main evidentiary points made in supporting paragraphs one and two.

This essay must be posted to Google Class by 11:59 pm tonight.

Day 10

Learners will provide at least one peer review according to the following criteria:

Rubric

The peer reviewed here posted their essay to Google Class by 11:59 pm of Day 9. **(0-20 points)**

The peer reviewed here had the following thesis statement: In some ways Sam Phillips, Johnny Cash, and Elvis Pressley are emblematic of the American Dream but in other ways their lives underscore the racial component that was deeply enmeshed in ideas of the American Dream. **(0-10 points)**

The peer's opening paragraph established the structure of the essay and defines "American Dream" according to the knowledge gained during Days 1 – 4. **(0-20 points)**

The peer's first supporting paragraph began with a topic sentence that supported the first part of the thesis statement (In some ways Sam Phillips, Johnny Cash, and Elvis Pressley are emblematic of the American Dream) and used evidence learned during the course of the project to support the topic sentence was used. **(0-20 points)**

The peer's second supporting paragraph began with a topic sentence that supported the second part of the thesis statement (Cash, Pressley, and Phillips' lives underscore the racial component that was deeply enmeshed in ideas of the American Dream) and used evidence learned during the course of the project to support their answer. **(0-20 points)**

The essay reviewed here concluded by restating the thesis and highlighting some of the main evidentiary points made in supporting paragraphs one and two. **(0-20 points)**

Total score _____

Project 10

"The Beat as an Object of Celebration and Scorn"

Overview: Learners will investigate some of the ways listeners feel and relate to rhythms, focusing on the language used to describe "the beat," and the manners in which rhythms connect to a deeper past and seem to anticipate particular futures. If "the beat" was a concern in 1950s America, it was again a concern for some, decades later, when Gangsta Rap began to dominate the Billboard charts. This project gets to the heart of the conflicts that arise as particular rhythms get made, released, listened to, and loved. With Little Richard as a focal figure, this project compels learners to explore the ways in which the rhythms in Little Richard's music elicited a strong response from teenage fans but also from pro-segregation forces. Equating "the beat" with a particular racial spirit and power, pro-segregationists railed against Rock and Roll as McCarthy railed against Communism.

Objectives: By the end of the project, learners will know the history of Senator Joseph McCarthy's campaigns against communism. Learners will know statistics regarding televisions in American households in the 1950s and the significance of those figures. Learners will know of "the beat" as a contested subject in American life. Learners will know about Jim Crow laws and their effects in 1950s America. Learners will know about musician Little Richard's roots and importance as an African-American Rock and Roll musician. Learners will know about "covers" of African-American music recorded by white musicians in the 1950s. Learners will know how opposition to Rock and Roll music in the 1950s sometimes focused on "the beat" and its connection to African-American culture. Learners will also be able to characterize social, economic, and cultural change over time. Learners will be able to interpret how public reaction to popular music reflects the social norms and values of a particular historical era. Learners will be able to analyze statements from historical materials to arrive at a better understanding of the past. Learners will be able to understand connections between popular culture and the time, place and social circumstances in which it was created. Learners will be able to integrate and evaluate information presented visually, quantitatively, and orally in diverse media and formats.

Essential Questions: How has "the beat" been an object of both celebration and concern in the history of popular music? How does that struggle around a contested issue such as "the beat" reveal itself, and how is it managed? And how can we study the past to learn more about the future we're making and the music we'll make it with?

Grade: High School and University

Subject: History, Social Studies, ELA, General Music

Estimated Time: 5 class sessions (45 – 50-minute classes)

Day 1

The project manager is advised to begin the project by presenting to learners the following:

Postwar America often appears to have been a conservative decade. The image of what might be called the "ideal American" circulated widely through the popularity of fifties television shows such as *Father Knows Best, The Ozzie and Harriet Show*, and other such family programming. The image these programs quietly promoted was that of a white, suburban family life in which gender roles were fixed and difficulties were few. Issues of racial discrimination, Cold War anxiety, and, really, conflict of any substantial kind was left at the door of television's dream world. Alternately, in that same time period

Senator Joe McCarthy's campaign to stamp out the "Communist threat" also promoted a vision of "the ideal American." But in McCarthy's case, he established a vision of the "ideal American" by arguing what one should not be if one wanted to attain such an ideal. Senator McCarthy used his political position to rail against the possibility of Communists "hidden in plain sight," going on to associate Communism with whatever else he believed to be "deviant" behavior. His list of those who threatened American life included anyone with an interest in Socialist ideas but also artists, homosexuals, labor organizers, and more. Ultimately deemed a "witch hunt," McCarthy's campaign to rid America of "Un-American activity" was one in which fear of the Other threatened to undo the principles of democracy as many Americans understood them. But in some fashion, McCarthy's anxieties, extreme in nature, were not his alone. McCarthy's "witch hunt" and its seemingly unlikely success as a political effort revealed the intolerance and anxiety about Otherness that was indeed a part of American life. Widespread concerns about the categories "normal" and "abnormal," "American" and "Un-American," "insider" and "outsider" revealed themselves across the fabric of the country. Into that historical moment came Rock and Roll. Rock and Roll included the music of groundbreaking African-American artists such as Fats Domino, Chuck Berry, and Little Richard, whose up-tempo, Southern, church-inspired beats caught the attention of both fans and those who worried that in these beats were the seeds of a kind of deviance that might itself be a threat. In that way, it was a time in which "the beat" became an issue in and of itself. This lesson explores the manner in which "the beat" in music has at different historical moments become a matter of contestation and anxious scrutiny. In 1950s America, it happened with Rock and Roll.

After presenting the information above, have learners to respond to the following:

- In music, what is a beat?
- What do you think of when I say "a beat" or "the beat" in relation to music?

Direct learners to focus on the sound of the beats they hear throughout the montage of popular music from different eras when watching "The Beat Throughout American Popular Music History": The Beat Throughout American Popular Music History - TeachRock

Compel learners to respond to the following:

- In the montage of music from the 1960s through the present in this clip, in what ways did you hear "the beat" change? Did it change drastically, or did you hear elements of "the beat" that remained somewhat constant throughout?

Next, introduce learners to Reverend Jimmie Snow, an anti-Rock and Roll preacher from the 1950s: Preaching Against Rock and Roll - TeachRock

Have learners respond to the following:

- Why do you think Jimmie Snow was concerned about "the beat"?
- Reverend Snow seems to believe "the beat" is capable of causing something to happen, what do you think he is afraid of?
- Why do you think Snow and others might have been concerned about the effect of "the beat" on young people in particular?
- Is there a "Jimmie Snow" in our contemporary world?

Day 2

Distribute to learners "The Media and Mainstream Culture in the 1950s": *Handout 1 - The Media and Mainstream Culture in the 1950s (teachrock.wpenginepowered.com)

Read aloud as a class. Help learners imagine what many historians have described as the generally conservative cultural climate of the 1950s. Then work through the questions at the bottom of the handout together. Then apprise learners of Little Richard, a queer African-American performer whose 1955 singles garnered national attention from multiracial audiences. Then play "Tutti Frutti" (1957) Tutti Frutti - TeachRock

Then ask:

- How would you describe the beat of "Tutti Frutti"?
- In what ways might you describe Little Richard's energy as a performer?

Then direct learners to write down the words they hear used to describe the beat and rhythms of Richard's music while they listen/watch the following clip: Describing the Beat of Little Richard - TeachRock

After the clip compel learners to respond to the following:

- What words did you hear used to describe Little Richard's beat?
- What do these terms suggest about how the music was perceived?
- How do you think Jimmie Snow might respond to the terminology used to describe Little Richard's beat?
- How do you think this music might fit into the idealized family worlds of *Leave it to Beaver* or *Father Knows Best*?
- Considering what you've seen so far in this lesson from television in the 1950s, what did Little Richard represent that most Americans were not seeing on TV

Next, distribute to learners a handout titled "Jim Crow and Musical Integration": *Handout 2 - Jim Crow and Musical Integration (teachrock.wpenginepowered.com)

Read the document aloud as a class then have learners respond to the following:

- In what ways might have Little Richard's popularity, especially his appearances on TV, disrupted nearly century-old Jim Crow laws?
- How did the White Citizens Council feel about Rock and Roll? For what aspects of Rock and Roll does the WCC express distaste? What do they say about it?
- Why do you think the White Citizens Council focused on "the beat" of Rock and Roll?
- The White Citizens Council suggested that Rock and Roll would "mongrelize" America. What is a "mongrel"? What do you think the WCC might have meant by this?

Explain to the class that there were many responses to Little Richard and other black musicians, both positive and negative, and not all of which were as direct as the statement by the White Citizens Council. Then play Pat Boone's rendition of "Tutti Frutti": Pat Boone's "Tutti Frutti" - TeachRock

Next, compel learners to respond to the following:

- Why do you think Pat Boone released a cover of "Tutti Frutti" so soon after Richard released his own version? What purposes do the people in this clip suggest Boone's cover of the song served?

- Thinking back to what you've seen and heard of Little Richard and Pat Boone, what was visually different about Boone's performance?
- Would you describe Boone's beat as "visceral" or "contagious"? If not, what adjectives would you use?
- Why might this performance have seemed "safer" to White parents or even Jimmie Snow? Which performer do you think would have been more likely to appear on *Father Knows Best*?
- Would Boone's performance have eased the White Citizen Councils' fears of "mongrelization"? How so?

Day 3

Explain to learners that, at the time, the association between "the beat" and black music meant that the beat was a lightning rod for anxieties around race. "The beat" seemed to have the potential to bring whatever stereotypes about Black culture a "concerned" White citizen harbored. It was "contagious," and the WCC was worried about who might "catch" it. Then have learners respond to the following questions:

- In the midst of concerns over segregation, why do you think "the beat" is what received the most attention from segregationists?
- Given all you've just heard about "the beat" from the earliest days of American history until the time of Little Richard, what do you think "the beat," as well as the dancing, feelings and reactions associated with it, represented to people like Jimmie Snow or organizations like the WCC?

Have learners break into six groups. Using the quotes below as a guide, groups one through three will argue on behalf of Little Richard. Groups four through six will argue on behalf of Pat Boone.

Distribute or display the following quotes.

Little Richard: "When 'Tutti Frutti' came out… They needed a rock star to block me out of white homes because I was a hero to white kids. The white kids would have Pat Boone up on the dresser and me in the drawer 'cause they liked my version better, but the families didn't want me because of the image that I was projecting."

Groups one through three must all craft a position paper supporting Richard's assertion, citing textual evidence (including videos) used during the course of the project.

Pat Boone: "Here's the bottom line. [In 1955] there were lots of rhythm and blues artists and they were doing well in their genre and they were famous and they had [album sales] charts and everything. The only ones that anyone knows today are the ones that were covered. By the Beatles, by Elvis, by me, by many artists…it introduced them to a far larger audience that they didn't have any access to at that point."

Groups four through six must all craft a position paper supporting Boone's assertion, citing textual evidence (including videos) used during the course of the project.

Day 4

Present learners with the RADAR method of revision. Encourage the groups to flesh out and revise their position papers. The paper must be posted to the Googe Class stream by 11:59 pm tonight.

Day 5

Have the class break into two debate teams and argue their points, citing evidence. Pick a winning team based on the use of evidence deployed in presenting their case. Consider awarding a prize (such as extra credit) and/or certificate to the winning team.

Project 11

"Music of the Civil Rights Movement"

Overview: Learners will explore the emergence of Sixties Soul music within the context of the Civil Rights movement of the early 1960s. Using Curtis Mayfield and the Impressions' iconic "People Get Ready" as a starting point, learners will examine the connection between musical and political voices, and the ways in which popular song helped express the values of the movement and served as a galvanizing force for those involved. Learners will also explore the relationship between music and the Civil Rights Movement. They will examine the development of the music within the movement and discover how that music helped organize the movement. Additionally, learners will identify how singing songs served as a nonviolent protest tactic that characterized the movement. Learners will discuss video clips, examine song lyrics and quotes, and analyze freedom songs to determine how music contributed to the success of the Civil Rights Movement. Learners will also explore learner-led efforts to end Jim Crow segregation during the Civil Rights Movement by examining significant events and identifying the unique role of music in calling people to action.

Objectives: Upon completion of this project, learners will know the contributions of such pioneering figures as Curtis Mayfield, Andrew Young, the Freedom Riders, and Martin Luther King Jr. to the Civil Rights movement and the emergence of Sixties Soul music. Learners will know the central importance of music to the progress of the Civil Rights movement. Learners will know the historical connection between religious and political themes both in the Civil Rights movement and in Sixties Soul. Learners will also develop interpretive skills by analyzing song lyrics and by identifying connections between artistic expression and the broader social and political context in which that expression occurs. By the end of the project, learners will know the essential role of music and singing during the Civil Rights Movement. Learners will know the African American history and culture of the music sung during the movement. Learners will know how music served as an organizational tool. Learners will know how singing was an act of nonviolent protest. Learners will know important figures in the Civil Rights Movement. Learners will also be able to articulate the role of music and singing songs during the Civil Rights Movement by watching video clips, examining primary sources, and analyzing music. By the end of the project, learners will also know historic moments of learner activism during the Civil Rights Movement, the unique role of music in learner-led school activism, how music can be used as an organizing tool. Learners will also know important figures, events, and learner organizations of the Civil Rights Movement. Learners will also be able to articulate the role of learner activism during the Civil Rights Movement by watching video clips, examining primary sources, and analyzing music.

Essential Question: How did Sixties Soul help give voice to the Civil Rights movement? How did music advance the goals and inform the tactics of the Civil Rights Movement? How did activism by Black learners challenge Jim Crow segregation during the Civil Rights Movement, and what unique role did music play as an organizing tool?

Grade: High School and University

Subject: History, Social Studies, ELA, General Music

Estimated Time: 10 class sessions (45 – 50-minute classes)

Day 1

The project manager is advised to begin the project by presenting the following information to the class:

The Civil Rights Movement of the mid-20th century was inextricably linked to music. The songs that Civil Rights activists sang became collectively known as *Freedom Songs*. Freedom Songs articulated the committed spirit and progressive themes of the movement. And since they were sung together by large masses of people, freedom songs demonstrated the organized group solidarity that was essential to the movement. But freedom songs were also sung by activists for many other reasons; to assuage their fears, to summon their courage, to express their joy, and as an act of nonviolent protest. Most Freedom Songs, and the themes expressed therein, were developed from African American Spirituals. Spirituals are a type of religious song created by enslaved African Americans in the southern U.S. that blended African musical elements and European church hymns. The use of Spirituals as the basis for Freedom Songs demonstrates the movement's origins in and development out of the Black Church, and the Church's cultural legacy within African American history. Perhaps no song is more closely associated with the Civil Rights Movement than "We Shall Overcome." With musical roots in numerous traditional Spirituals and hymns, its ubiquitous use in the movement can be traced back to the labor movement of the 1940s, as an early version of "We Shall Overcome" was sung by striking Black tobacco workers. But "We Shall Overcome" was not the only freedom song sung. Dozens of Freedom Songs were developed out of Spirituals, and more contemporary Gospel and popular music songs, and the lyrics were frequently modified to suit a particular moment in the movement. Folk musicians like Odetta helped popularize Freedom Songs within the movement and throughout American society. As the profile of the Civil Rights Movement grew, popular music singer-songwriters like Sam Cooke wrote new Freedom Songs that reflected the themes of the movement, and their personal experience of racism as African Americans and offered inspiration and encouragement for transcending the hardship of oppression. Regardless of the origins or the person singing the song, Freedom Songs profoundly informed the Civil Rights Movement by serving as an organizational tool, a protest tactic, and an artistic expression of the myriad of emotions and intentions of the movement.

After the presentation, present any rubrics that might be used to evaluate learners' performance during the course of the project. Then divide the class into pairs for a Think-Pair-Share activity. Ask the following question:

- Why do people sing?

Compel learners to write down one or two ideas that come to mind, then share/compare answers with a partner. The project manager may wish to offer the following examples to help encourage a wide range of learner responses: a child joins a church choir, your brother sings in the shower, slaves sang work songs and "field hollers" while they harvested cotton, a mother sings a child to sleep. Next, ask for pairs to share their ideas with the class. Post sample answers on the board. Then, discuss the following:

- Do people sing for one reason?
- Can someone be singing for more than one reason at the same time? What might be an example of this?
- Why do you think it has been so important for people to sing no matter the time they lived in or the circumstances they faced?
- Does singing change things? Why or why not?

Distribute to each group a handout about Andrew Young: Microsoft Word - Handout 1.doc (teachrock.wpenginepowered.com)

Have each group read the handout. Then play Young discussing Curtis Mayfield's "People Get Ready": The Impact of Curtis Mayfield and the Impressions on the Civil Rights Movement - TeachRock

Distribute a handout about "People Get Ready": Microsoft Word - peoplegetready.edited.doc (teachrock.org)

Play the video for "People Get Ready": People Get Ready - TeachRock

Have learners follow along with the lyrics and then respond to the following:

- Ask each pair to discuss briefly what they think the song is about. After they've done this, ask each learner to write one sentence summarizing in his or her own words what the song is about.

Poll sample learner responses. Then lead a class-wide discussion built around the following questions:

- Is "People Get Ready" a religious song? What might be some clues suggesting religious themes?
- Is "People Get Ready" about something other than religion? What might that be?
- What does the song mean when it says you "don't need no baggage" and "don't need no ticket"? To go where?
- Whom do you think this song would most appeal to?
- Why do you think this became such an important song in the Civil Rights movement, as Young discussed?

Have each group read the excerpt from the project essay about the song, alternating by paragraph. Have them underline key words and phrases as they read and listen. Then discuss the following with the class:

- What does the author believe made Mayfield's music so important to the Civil Rights movement?

Day 2

Distribute to learners a handout pertaining to "Freedom Riders and Song": Microsoft Word - Handout 3-Freedom Riders and Song.doc (teachrock.wpenginepowered.com)

Also distribute this writing prompt: Microsoft Word - soulexitticket.edited.doc (teachrock.wpenginepowered.com)

Then watch the clip of Martin Luther King Jr. on the "Merv Griffen Show" (1967): The Merv Griffin Show - TeachRock

Then have learners respond to the following:

- What do you feel are the main points Dr. King makes?
- What is his explanation for violence at Civil Rights demonstrations?
- How would you describe his manner in this casual, talk-show context?

Watch the clip of Rosa Parks discussing the Civil Rights Movement: Civil Rights - TeachRock

Learners are to write an account of what happened to Parks based on her retelling, using your own words. Have learners complete their writing prompt and turn it in.

Day 3

Give learners the rest of the day to research why Martin Luther King was jailed in Birmingham, Alabama in 1963. And have them read King's seminal "Letter From Birmingham Jail": Handout-1-Dr.-Martin-Luther-King-Letter-From-Birmingham-Jail.pdf (teachrock.wpenginepowered.com)

As an exit ticket, have learners turn in an explanation for why king was jailed, what inspired his letter, and who the letter was addressed to (and why them), and what the mood and tone of the letter is.

Day 4

Play the "The Black Church": The Black Church (youtube.com)

Then ask learners to respond to the following:

- In what ways has the Black Church shaped African American and American history?
- What role did the Church play in the Civil Rights Movement?
- What "musical legacy" was the source for many of the songs of the Civil Rights Movement? Who created that musical legacy?
- Did you recognize the song being sung in the video when Reverend Dr. Martin Luther King Jr. was introduced? If so, what's the title of the song?

Distribute "We Shall Overcome": Handout-We-Shall-Overcome.pdf (teachrock.wpenginepowered.com)

Solicit volunteers to read the introduction and lyrics aloud. Then have learners respond to the following:

- What are the cultural and religious origins of "We Shall Overcome"?
- What are the songs that civil rights activists sang collectively known as?

Play "We Shall Overcome": We Shall Overcome - TeachRock

Instruct learners to read along (or sing along) with the lyrics. Inform the class that the singing is led by the Freedom Singers, a music group of learner Civil Rights activists. Then ask:

- What instruments are performing the music? What do you hear? What is absent?
- What is the term for performing music solely with voices, without musical instrument accompaniment?
- What might be the benefits of singing music without instruments?
- What are some of the themes expressed in the lyrics? How might the congressional singing and the themes expressed in the lyrics be representative of African American history?
- How does the song make you feel? Why might the song make you feel that way?
- What emotions and thoughts does it arouse? Why might the song bring up those emotions and thoughts?

Play "Georgia Stories: Singing Freedom": The Civil Rights Movement: Singing Freedom | Georgia Stories - YouTube

Then have learners respond to the following:

- According to Charles Sherrod, what strategy was used to fight Jim Crow segregation during the Civil Rights Movement?
- What words does Rutha Mae Harris use to describe what Freedom Songs and singing did for those participating in the movement?
- How were traditional African American spirituals modified to become Freedom Songs?
- Were there any themes you noticed in the songs sung in the video? If so, what were they?

Day 5

Explain to the class that each group will work together to analyze a particular freedom song from the Civil Rights Movement. Inform learners that during their analysis, they will be: discovering the song's origins, identifying lyrical themes, and comparing and contrasting the song with other Freedom Songs.

Distribute: Station-Activity-Keep-Your-Eyes-on-the-Prize.pdf (teachrock.wpenginepowered.com)

Play "Eyes on the Prize": Keep Your Eyes on the Prize - TeachRock

Have learners answer the questions in the packet.

Distribute: Station-Activity-This-Little-Light-of-Mine.pdf (teachrock.wpenginepowered.com)

Play "This Little Light of Mine": This Little Light of Mine - TeachRock

Have learners answer the questions in the packet.

Distribute: Station-Activity-Oh-Freedom.pdf (teachrock.wpenginepowered.com)

Play "Oh Freedom": Oh Freedom (youtube.com)

Have learners answer the questions in the packet.

Distribute: Station-Activity-A-Change-is-Gonna-Come.pdf (teachrock.wpenginepowered.com)

Play "A Change is Gonna Come": A Change is Gonna Come - TeachRock

Conclude by having learners respond to the following:

- How does the song's history in the Civil Rights Movement inform your understanding of the movement?

Play a clip of the Freedom Singers performing: The Freedom Singers Perform at the White House: 8 of 11 - YouTube

Distribute: Handout-Music-of-the-Civil-Rights-Movement.pdf (teachrock.wpenginepowered.com)

Read the text aloud and encourage learners to circle any words and phrases that they recognize and any that they do not. Then ask:

- Why was music so important to the Civil Rights Movement?
- What does Bernice Johnson Reagon suggest music could provide for the movement? What does she suggest music could provide for participants in the movement?
- How can music help someone or some issue "become visible"?
- Is music simply a form of entertainment, or can it have other purposes as well?

Day 6

The project manager is advised to scaffold the next phase in the project by presenting the following information to the class:

During the 1960s, Shelley "The Playboy" Stewart played new hit records by current artists on Birmingham, Alabama's WENN radio station. So, when he played Big Joe Turner's 1954 hit song "Shake, Rattle and Roll" one day in May 1963, it sounded out of place. Stewart intended it that way. Stewart wasn't simply playing an "oldie" for his listeners. He was using music as an organizing tool to call people to action, particularly young people. On May 2, 1963, hundreds of Black learners in Birmingham boycotted school and marched downtown to protest the city's pervasive Jim Crow laws, laws that included racially segregating the public schools that those same learners attended. Earlier that day, Sterns played "Shake, Rattle and Roll" to send a covert message to his organized learner listeners: it's time to rally. Nearly ten years earlier in 1954, the same year "Shake, Rattle and Roll" was a No. 1 hit, the U.S. Supreme Court unanimously ruled in *Brown v. Board of Education of Topeka* that segregation in public schools was unconstitutional. In the ruling, the Court instructed all public schools to desegregate but did not specify a deadline. This historic ruling reversed the long-standing legal doctrine of "separate but equal," which had determined that racially segregating public schools was constitutional. Under "separate but equal," as long as a segregated school attended by Black learners was equal in quality to a segregated school attended by white learners, racial segregation was not violating the Equal Protection Clause of the U.S. Constitution. In reality, while segregation had led to an American society that was racially separated, inequality was widespread and disenfranchised Black communities. The inferior quality of the public schools attended by Black learners was a glaring example, and the *Brown* ruling in 1954 acknowledged it. Unfortunately, segregation in public schools endured even after the Supreme Court declared it unconstitutional due to local and state resistance, which was why in 1963 learners in Birmingham were marching in protest. But this was not the first time that learners had protested the inequality of segregated public schools. In the early 1950s, years before the *Brown* ruling, Black learners in segregated schools organized and led walkouts and strikes to protest substandard school facilities and education resources. The purpose of their activism was not necessarily to desegregate schools but rather to attend schools that were as equally equipped as those of their white counterparts – the equality in "separate but equal." Their actions produced results: improved school facilities, recognition of their efforts by the media, and support from the National Association for the Advancement of Colored People (NAACP). Black learner activism directly informed the NAACP's legal strategy in challenging "separate but equal" in court during the early 1950s. The NAACP included a 1951 learner walkout and strike in Virginia as one of the cases in their class-action lawsuit that eventually became the historic *Brown* case. Working with the NAACP, future Supreme Court Justice Thurgood Marshall was the lead attorney that successfully argued *Brown* before the Court. However, even as local and state resistance allowed school segregation to endure, learner activism continued to challenge it into the 1960s. Learner activism during the Civil Rights Movement also confronted racial segregation in other public spaces. In early 1960, Black college learners began "sit-in" demonstrations to protest segregation in restaurants. Out of that action, the Learner Nonviolent Coordinating Committee (SNCC) was founded. The SNCC (more-commonly pronounced, *Snick*) was formed under the mentoring of Civil Rights Movement leader, Ella Baker. A decades-long veteran of the movement, Baker encouraged young people to recognize their own leadership capabilities and assemble their own independent organizations. With singing being so important to the

Civil Rights Movement, SNCC members formed the Freedom Singers music group. The group traveled around the U.S., performing concerts to raise funds for the SNCC and to inform their audiences about Civil Rights organizing happening around the country. The Freedom Singers activism and performances demonstrated another example of music as an organizing tool during the Civil Rights Movement. The group sang at, and the SNCC helped organize, the March on Washington for Jobs and Freedom in Washington, DC on August 28, 1963. Notably, at the March, current SNCC National Chairman, and future congressman, John Lewis delivered remarks before the enormous crowd and later in the day Dr. Martin Luther King Jr. gave his famous "I Have a Dream" speech.

After presenting the information above, the project manager is advised to play a bit of video on *Brown v. Board of Education of Topeka, Kansas*: Brown v. Board of Education of Topeka - TeachRock

Compel learners to respond to the following:

- Why were schools segregated?
- According to the video, where was segregation "outlawed"?
- What branch of the U.S. government "outlawed" segregation and what year did it happen?
- How did learners contribute to *Brown v. Board of Education of Topeka*? How might learners have contributed to the Civil Rights Movement in general?

Explain to learners that they will be examining how young people organized to protest racial segregation before and after the *Brown v. Board of Education* ruling, and how music served as an organizing tool for their protests.

Distribute to learners: Handout-Learner-Activism-Station-Activity-Guide_V2.pdf (teachrock.wpenginepowered.com)

Then organize learners into four groups and assign a station for each group to visit. Explain to the groups that at their station they will read an overview of the event, read a song title and a brief excerpt of the song's lyrics, and view record covers of the song's performers. They will then complete the Station Activity Guide and choose a song that they feel best matches with their Civil Rights learner activism event.

Station 1: Learner Activism in Farmville, Virginia in 1951: Station-1-Materials-Learner-Activism-in-Farmville-Virginia-in-1951_V2.pdf (teachrock.wpenginepowered.com)

Station 2: Learner Activism in Kinston, North Carolina in 1951: Station-2-Materials-Learner-Activism-in-Kinston-North-Carolina_V2.pdf (teachrock.wpenginepowered.com)

Station 3: Learner Activism in Birmingham, Alabama in 1963: Station-3-Materials-Learner-Activism-in-Birmingham-Alabama_V2.pdf (teachrock.wpenginepowered.com)

Station 4: Learner Activism in New York, New York in 1964: Station-4-Materials-Learner-Activism-in-New-York-New-York_V2.pdf (teachrock.wpenginepowered.com)

Once each group has visited each station, bring the class back together to share their answers to the comprehension questions and explain their song selection using the lyrics as evidence. Next, explain to learners that now they will be examining learner organizations during the Civil Rights Movement and how music served as an organizing tool. Then have them respond to the following:

- Do you think racial segregation was happening in places beyond schools at this time? What sorts of places?
- Do you think learners protested at these other places? How might have they protested?

Day 7

Play a video on the sit-in movement: The Sit-In Movement (youtube.com)

Have learners respond to the following:

- Who started the sit-in movement?
- Where did it begin?
- How did a sit-in take place? What was the purpose of a sit-in?
- What new learner organization helped the sit-in movement?

Distribute: Handout-Learner-Nonviolent-Coordinating-Committee-SNCC.pdf (teachrock.wpenginepowered.com)

Read the text aloud and have learners circle any words and phrases that they recognize and any that they do not. Then ask learners to respond to the following:

- How did the SNCC interact with the SCLC and Reverend Dr. Martin Luther King Jr.?
- Why might the SNCC have taken their independent approach?
- What veteran civil rights organizer and SCLC official encouraged the founding of the SNCC?

Play clip about Ella Baker: Ella Baker - 'The Mother of the Civil Rights Movement' - YouTube

Have learners respond to the following:

- For what reason is Ella Baker known as "The Mother of the Civil Rights Movement"?
- What advice did she give members of the SNCC when they visited rural areas promoting Civil Rights?
- What did she encourage young people in the Civil Rights Movement to do?

Day 8

Watch this *Voices of the Civil Rights Movement* clip to discover more about the Children's Crusade in Birmingham, AL in May 1963: Black Children Arrested & Assaulted in Birmingham - YouTube

Have learners take notes while listening to Alabama's Public Radio's "Civil Rights Radio" to learn about the role Black DJs played in fostering the Civil Rights Movement: Alabama Public Radio-- "Civil Rights Radio" | Alabama Public Radio (apr.org)

Read about the "Teens Take Charge Learner Activism" Event at a New York City school in 2019 to identify how school segregation endures: NYC learners walk out of class, pledging weekly strikes to demand integration - Chalkbeat

Day 9

Divide the class into groups of no more than four people per group. Explain to learners that they are going to take on the role of a youth-led social rights organization. Each group is tasked with:

- Choose a contemporary cause of their choice.
- Choosing an organized action to call attention to their cause (for example: a school walkout, school boycott, sit-in, or another nonviolent action).
- Choosing a song that represents their cause and could be used as an organizing tool to signal learners to action.
- Groups are to consider Cause, Action, and Songs.

Ask groups to share their choices and list them using the following prompts:

- What would be your cause? Why?
- What would be your method of action? Why?
- What song would represent your cause and be used as an organizing tool? Why?
- Create a learner activism playlist comprised of at least seven songs.

The groups need to provide some insight into how the history explored in this project might have informed the cause chosen by the group, the group's method of action, and each song on the playlist?

Day 10

Groups present their Cause, Action, and Songs and some explanation of why they chose their particular songs on their playlist. Learners will also provide peer reviews of groupmates according to the following criteria:

__Rubric__

The groupmate took part in deciding on the "cause" the group addressed. **(0-10 points)**

The groupmate took part in devising a "plan of action" to address the cause. **(0-10 points)**

The groupmate took part in finding at least one song for the playlist and explained why the song(s) makes sense for the cause/action plan devised by the group. **(0-10 points)**

The groupmate took part in presenting information to the rest of the class derived from the input in regards to the group's cause, action plan, and playlist. **(0-10 points)**

The groupmate was ready, willing, and able to present when called upon. **(0-10 points)**

The groupmate took part in establishing how the presentation was informed by information learned during the course of this project. **(0-10 points)**

Total score _____

Project 12

"The Counterculture"

Overview: Learners will explore the significance of the Haight-Ashbury in the 1960s by watching clips from the documentary *Long Strange Trip* and reading journalistic accounts of the hippie movement in that neighborhood. Learners will also address the significance of the countercultural scene.

Objectives: By the end of the project, learners will know the "mainstream" social and cultural environment of the 1960s. Learners will know the dominant beliefs and actions of the counterculture of the late 1960s. Learners will know the writing of Herbert Marcuse. Learners will know the historical significance of San Francisco's Haight-Ashbury neighborhood. Learners will know journalistic accounts of Haight-Ashbury by Ralph J. Gleason, Tom Wolfe, Joan Didion, Hunter S. Thompson, and Warren Hinckle. Learners will also be able to define the idea of "counterculture" and contextualize the concept in the present moment by examining journalism, literature, and music of the 1960s.

Essential Questions: How did the counterculture movement of the late 1960s challenge traditional American behaviors and values, and how did the Grateful Dead reflect these changing views of life and society? Were hippies trying to change American society, or simply escape it?

Grade: High School and University

Subject: History, Social Studies, ELA, General Music

Estimated Time: 7 class sessions (45 – 50-minute classes)

Day 1

The project manager is advised to present all or some of the following information in an effort to scaffold for learners the project:

After World War II, The United States entered into a period of enormous economic growth and prosperity that lasted until the early 1970s. While the war was over, the perceived threat of communism resulted in escalated military spending, which led to the development of many new technologies and industries. In addition, the U.S. government continued to invest in social projects such as public schools, housing, highways, welfare, and veterans benefits that stimulated growth. Unions, a major influence in the US labor market following the support of the Franklin D. Roosevelt administration, were able to successfully negotiate fair wages for workers. As a result, millions of Americans gained access to meaningful employment, invested in homes, and stocked them with families and new commodities. After a long period of declining births, the post-World War II era saw the birth rate skyrocket and the nation's population rose almost 20 percent. The generation now known as the "Baby Boomer" was born. There were some, however, who were troubled by the consumption during this "Golden Era of Capitalism." Perhaps the most poignant and detailed critiques came from a group of German scholars collectively known as the Frankfurt School. Having experienced the Holocaust first-hand, Frankfurt School critics like Herbert Marcuse, Max Horkheimer, and Theodor Adorno feared that the consumerist society of the 1950s wasn't liberating people, but rather acting as a means of social control. For them, TV shows, popular music, and the newest dishwasher were nothing more than a way to placate the masses, and keep the average Westerner distracted and uninterested in thinking critically about rampant militarization and a world that was spiraling ever closer to nuclear war. By the time the Baby Boom generation was coming into adulthood in the mid-1960s, the Frankfurt School's criticisms had begun to garner more attention. Many of the young adult "Boomers" became disenchanted with the types of consumption valued by their parents' generation and began seeking new experiences, experimenting with varied modes of thought and styles of living. One of the most famous of such experiments culminated at Haight-Ashbury, a district of San Francisco, California. Between 1965 and 1967, young people from across the country arrived to Haight-Ashbury, drawn in by cheap rent and the bohemian reputation of the neighborhood established largely by the various artists of the Beat era. A vibrant counterculture developed, made up of a community of what some would later refer to as "hippies," people who rejected the pressure to live as workers, earners, and consumers within a singular family unit. During this era, many in Haight-Ashbury embraced the possibilities of nearly anything perceived as outside the mainstream, including communism and communal living, open relationships and sexual liberation, various elements of Eastern religions, and psychotropic drugs such as LSD and peyote. And, of course, music. Rock and Roll was the primary musical language of Haight-Ashbury, and in the hands of its inhabitants, the music became experimental and careened outside its previous bounds. Free concerts proliferated in San Francisco's Golden Gate Park and on the city's streets, while venues such as the Matrix and the Fillmore showcased bands that personified the "San Francisco Sound": Jefferson Airplane, Quicksilver Messenger Service, Big Brother and the Holding Company, and others. The band that came to most represent this moment in Haight-Ashbury, however, was the Grateful Dead. While the Grateful Dead and their fans maintained some elements of countercultural ideals well into the 1990s, much of the idealism of Haight-Ashbury as a utopian location did not survive the 1960s. Following the publicity of the 1967 "Summer of Love," thousands flocked to the neighborhood, overrunning the area, and, in the language of the day, "burning out." American corporations saw the value of "flower power," and absorbed key elements of the movement for marketing purposes, turning much of it into nothing more than a fashion trend that could be found in stores across America. Record companies too saw opportunity, and some of the San Francisco bands ultimately became the Top-40 artists they were so critical of earlier in their careers. Some suggest that by the time the country embraced the counterculture, it was already over.

After presenting the information above to learners, present any rubrics that will be used to evaluate their performance during the course of the project. Then compel learners to respond to the following:

- Have you ever heard the term "counterculture" or "countercultural"? What do you think that term means?

Ask learners to write a 1-sentence definition of the term on a scratch piece of paper.

Show learners the actual definition to counterculture: "A way of life and set of attitudes opposed to or at variance with the prevailing social norm."

Then ask learners to respond to the following:

- Was your definition similar to the dictionary definition?
- How was your definition different than the dictionary definition?
- What might it mean to be "opposed to" or "at variance with" a social norm? Can you give an example?
- Can you think of an activity, attitude, or past-time that might be considered "countercultural" today? Why?
- To be against the social norm, you first have to define what the "social norm" is. What do you think some of the "social norms" are today? Where do you see them? How do you experience them?

Day 2

Inform learners that they will be exploring the social norms and countercultural movement of the 1960s. Then play a sampling of "TV Commercials From the 1960s and 1970s: <u>Television Commercials from the 1960s and 1970s - TeachRock</u>

Compel learners to take notes on what values they think these commercials promoted. Then ask them:

- What kinds of things are being sold in these commercials? What categories of products do they belong to?
- What kinds of audiences do you think these commercials might have been catering to? What different ways do you think they attempted to excite or interest their audiences?
- In what ways are these products being sold? What problems do the commercials suggest they might solve for customers?
- Do you think some of the commercials were catered more to men, and others to women? Why? Did the commercials use different approaches towards male audiences versus female audiences? What might this say about society in the 1960s?
- What sort of values might these commercials be promoting? Why?
- Are the commercials telling the audience to buy a product and/or suggesting to their audience that they should be and act a certain way?
- What else did you notice about the commercials?

Then inform learners that in the 1950s and 1960s, the US experienced an economic boom. For the first time, millions of people could afford their own house, and new technologies allowed a variety of goods to be produced cheaply. While many celebrated this era, others were critical, fearing Americans were becoming mindless workers and consumers incapable of critical thought. Then display for learners the following excerpt from *One-Dimensional Man*:

"Today people recognize themselves by their commodities; they find their soul in their automobile, hi fi set, split-level home, kitchen equipment."

"The means of mass transportation and communication, the commodities of lodging, food, and clothing, the irresistible output of the entertainment and information industries carry with them prescribed attitudes and habits... which bind the consumers more or less pleasantly to the producers"

"Thus emerges a pattern of one-dimensional thought and behavior in which ideas, aspirations, and objectives that ... transcend the established universe of discourse and action are either repelled or reduced to terms of this universe."

Inform learners that the above quotes come from the book *One-Dimensional Man,* by Herbert Marcuse. Written in 1964, the book became one of the most well-known texts that critiqued mainstream culture in the 1960s. Have learners respond to the following questions:

- What do you think Marcuse means by the word "commodities"? What kind of examples of commodities does he list?
- In the first except, what might Marcuse mean when he writes that "people recognize themselves by their commodities"? Can you think of an example of how someone could be recognized or defined by the things they buy?
- In the second excerpt, Marcuse argues that customers are bound to the producers that make the things they buy. In what way might this be the case? Do you feel a close connection with a particular company or brand? Why?

- In the second excerpt, Marcuse states that products "carry with them prescribed attitudes and habits." What sorts of attitudes and habits were reinforced by the commercials you watched earlier? What sort of habits might be associated with products today?
- In the third excerpt, what might the word "discourse" mean? What does he mean by the "universe of discourse?"
- How might consumerist society limit or control what people talk about or what they do on a daily basis, leading to "One-Dimensional Thought"? What might companies want their customers thinking about, and what might they not want their customers thinking about?
- To resist "One-Dimensional Thought," Marcuse recommends a "great refusal." How might one refuse consumer culture?

Day 3

Play for learners a clip introducing the Haight Ashbury: Introducing Haight-Ashbury - TeachRock

Compel learners to respond to the following:

- What was appealing to the "Hippies" about the neighborhood of Haight-Ashbury?
- The journalist describing Haight-Ashbury in the clip claims that the neighborhood attracted young people "seeking something new and significant for themselves." What might have these young people hoped to find?
- What might daily life have been like for the young people who relocated to the Haight-Ashbury neighborhood? Would you want to live in that kind of environment? Why or why not?
- How can moving to Haight-Ashbury be seen as its own "great refusal"? What might have these people have been refusing?

Play for learners a clip introducing the Grateful Dead: Introducing the Grateful Dead - TeachRock

Compel learners to respond to the following:

- What was the Grateful Dead's daily life like when they lived in Haight-Ashbury? Do you think this was typical of others who lived there?
- What might have Jerry Garcia meant when he said at the beginning of the clip, "We'd all like to be able to live an uncluttered life, a simple life, a good life?" How might that statement have been a critique of the mainstream society of the 1960s?
- How does the Grateful Dead's living situation differ from what was presented in the commercials? Do you think their lifestyle was common at the time? What might make their lifestyle "countercultural"?

Divide the class into groups of five, and pass out a PDF in which journalists describe the Haight-Ashbury Handout-1-Accounts-of-the-Haight-Ashbury-Scene.pdf (teachrock.wpenginepowered.com)

Compel learners to complete the instructions on the handout, and then report to the class the discussion they had and the conclusions they made as a group. Have groups specifically address the following:

- Based on what you read and watched today, can you summarize the philosophy of the Hippies and new young people in Haight-Ashbury? How could it be considered countercultural?
- What were the goals of the Hippie movement? How were those goals achieved? How were they frustrated?

- Do you think the Hippie movement brought about any change in American society or culture? If so, what sort of change? If not, how come?
- Do you see any contradictions within the varied goals of the people drawn to San Francisco?

Then display the excerpts from *One-Dimensional Man* again. Direct learners' attention to the first excerpt, and ask:

- Today, what sort of products might have Marcuse criticized? Would it still be cars, television sets, houses, and kitchen equipment, or would it be something else? What products today might Marcuse say people "find their soul" in?
- What would a "great refusal" look like today? Is it possible to be countercultural in today's society? What risks would it entail, and what benefits? Would it still look something like the Haight-Ashbury Hippie scene? Why or why not.

Play for learners some tunes by any or all of the bands that constructed the "San Francisco sound: Grateful Dead, Jefferson Airplane, Country Joe and the Fish, and Quicksilver Messenger Service.

Have learners summarize what they see as the defining characteristics of this style of music, and consider the ways those musical characteristics might represent the attitudes among the hippies in Haight-Ashbury.

Then have learners interview a classmate. Learners are to ask if the interviewee exemplifies the "counterculture" by delving into their beliefs and opinions of society.

Day 4

Have learners read Jia Tolentino's *New Yorker* article "Outdoor Voices Blurs the Lines Between Working Out and Everything Else": Outdoor Voices Blurs the Lines Between Working Out and Everything Else | The New Yorker

Learners are to write a short essay (300 to 400 words) discussing the ways Tolentino's account of "Outdoor Voices" compares and contrasts with Marcuse's critique of society in the 1960s.

The primary question learners need to consider is:

The essay must be structured as follows:

- Thesis statement with supporting structure of essay. The thesis must address the following question: Has much changed in consumerism since the 1960s?
- A supporting paragraph comparing and contrasting "Outdoor Voices" with Marcuse's critique of 1960s society.
- A supporting paragraph explaining how much (or not) consumerism has changed since the 1960s.
- A concluding paragraph that restates the thesis and highlights main ideas from supporting paragraphs.

Learners are to be provided the day to read the article, locate evidence to support their thesis, and outline their paper.

Day 5

Provide learners the day to craft their essay.

Day 6

Introduce learners to the RADAR revision method. Then provide learners the period to revise and solicit feedback from classmates. The essay must be posted to the Google Class stream by 11:59 pm tonight.

Day 7

Learners will provide at least two peer reviews according to the following criteria:

__Rubric__

The peer reviewed here submitted their essay to the Google Class stream by 11:59 pm of Day 6. **(0-20 points)**

The peer reviewed here wrote a 300 to 400 word-essay. **(0-20 points)**

The essay was free of spelling and grammar errors: **(0-10 points)**

The essay has a clear thesis statement. **(0-10 points)**

The thesis statement addresses the question: Has much changed in consumerism since the 1960s? **(0-20 points)**

The opening paragraph of the essay (after the thesis statement) delved into the structure of the essay. **(0-20 points)**

The first supporting paragraph compares and contrasts "Outdoor Voices" with Marcuse's critique of 1960s society. **(0-20 points)**

The second supporting paragraph explains how much (or not) consumerism has changed since the 1960s. **(0-20 points)**

The essay has a concluding paragraph that restates the thesis and highlights main ideas from supporting paragraphs. **(0-20 points)**

Total score _____

Project 13

"The Vietnam War Project"

Overview: Learners will examine ten primary source documents to consider the ways the United States' involvement in Vietnam affected the culture and values of the country. The goal of the project is to challenge learners to think critically and to consider viewpoints that are frequently inconsistent and contradictory. Learners will examine how Crosby, Stills, Nash, and Young's "Ohio," Merle Haggard's "Okie From Muskogee" and Edwin Starr's "War" articulated the divisive feelings Americans had about the war in the late 1960s and early 1970s. To supplement these songs, Learners will also watch clips from *CNN's* "Soundtracks" and analyze polling data, news articles, and photographs from the era. Participants in this project will learn how a number of songs released during and after the Vietnam War articulated the experiences of Americans who served in the United States Armed Forces during the war. Learners will analyze popular songs that have resonated with veterans, and many other Americans, since the time they were released. While analyzing the songs, Learners will examine newspaper editorials, first-hand accounts, and personal reflections from Vietnam veterans. Finally, learners will watch clips from the *CNN* "Soundtracks" series to provide additional context and information to inform their discussion and activities.

Objectives: Upon completion of this lesson, learners will know the changing media representation of war during the America's war in Vietnam. Learners will know the growing opposition of many citizens, particularly young Americans, to the Vietnam conflict in the 1960s. Learners will know the influence of the baby boom, popular media, and popular music of the antiwar movement. Learners will know the role of protest music in giving Americans who could not vote in the mid-1960s a public voice on political issues. Learners will know the passage of the 26th Amendment in 1971, lowering the voting age from 21 to 18. Learners will also be able to analyze and evaluate multiple historical sources, including images, statistics, videos, and music. Learners will be able practice literacy skills – reading, speaking, and writing. Learners will also be able understand music in relation to history and culture. Upon completion of this project, learners will know Sgt. Barry Sadler's "Ballad of the Green Beret," President Lyndon Johnson, The Gulf of Tonkin incident, Joe McDonald's "I-Feel-Like-I'm-Fixin'-to-Die Rag," Activist Paul Potter, the Weather Underground, Photographer Bernie Boston, The Inauguration of Richard Nixon, the Pentagon Papers, Journalist James Reston, and know Merle Haggard's "Okie from Muskogee." Learners will also evaluate the extent to which the Civil Rights Movement acted as a turning point in American history by analyzing a variety of historical documents. Learners will by the end of the project know seminal events during the Vietnam War, including the Gulf of Tonkin Resolution, The Tet Offensive, the My Lai Massacre, the election of Richard Nixon, and the Kent State shootings. Learners will know the feelings Americans had about the Vietnam War, including the division between the "Doves" and "Hawks." Learners will know the way popular music either directly contributed to discussions about the Vietnam War, or was appropriated by pro-and anti-Vietnam War groups. Learners will also be able to define the differing political viewpoints Americans had during the Vietnam War by examining the music, journalism, and photography of the era. Upon completion of this project, learners will know the diverse experiences and perspectives of American Vietnam War veterans. Learners will know how popular music connected Americans serving in Vietnam to life back home in the U.S. Learners will know particular songs that informed and represented the experience of Americans serving in the armed forces during the Vietnam War, and their life afterward in the U.S. as veterans. Learners will know how polarization toward the war affected U.S. service people in Vietnam, as it did American society in the U.S. Learners will also be able to develop a more nuanced awareness of the experiences and perspectives of Vietnam War veterans by exploring first-hand accounts, music, song lyrics, and video clips.

Essential Questions: In what ways and to what extent did the Vietnam War change American culture, society, and values? How were American's divisive opinions over the Vietnam War articulated by musicians in the 1960s and early 1970s? How did popular music amplify the voices and experiences of Americans serving in the United States Armed Forces during the Vietnam War?

Grade: High School and University

Subject: History, Social Studies, ELA, General Music

Estimated Time: 15 class sessions (45 – 50-minute classes)

Day 1

The project manager is advised to present to learners all or some of the following information:

In the years following World War II, a brief period of American euphoria gave way to fear of a new antagonist: communism. Though the U.S. and the Soviet Union were allies during the war, Soviet efforts to rebuild Eastern Europe in its own image led to an American fear of ever-spreading communism and caused a rift between the two countries. Allies no longer, the U.S. and the Soviet Union engaged in an indirect conflict known as the Cold War from 1947 until the communist government collapsed in 1991. Regardless of tensions, the United States and the Soviet Union, now the world's two nuclear superpowers, knew that a direct war would lead to "mutually assured destruction" in which both countries would lose. Therefore, each nation sought to pursue its aims "by proxy" in other nations. In 1956, with the aid of the Soviets, the League for the Independence of Vietnam overthrew the U.S.-supported French colonial government in Vietnam, leaving the country divided into a Soviet-backed communist North and U.S.-backed republic South. Fighting erupted between the two sides in the early 1960s. What began as an envoy of U.S. "advisors" to South Vietnam in 1964 quickly escalated, and by 1969, 500,000 U.S. troops were involved in the conflict. As the American body count rose–nearly 17,000 U.S. soldiers died in 1968 alone–Americans became divided on the war's merit. The pro-war "Hawks" feared loss in Vietnam would signal a victory for the Soviet Union, and that protecting the United States from the perceived "communist threat," wherever it might appear, was one's patriotic duty. The anti-war "Doves" felt the war was barbaric, and the casualties on both sides served little to no purpose. In 1970, division over the Vietnam War reached a point of crises: in May that year, the National Guard shot and killed four anti-war protesters at Kent State University. Today, the tragedy at Kent State might not be best remembered through a news article, but a song: Crosby, Stills, Nash, and Young's "Ohio," which powerfully articulates the moment when the violence of the Vietnam War was turned inward, upon American learners. But "Ohio," was one of many songs in the 1960s and 1970s that signified the cultural division between the Hawks and Doves.

After the presentation, present learners with any rubrics that might be used to evaluate their performance during the course of this project. Then distribute to learners the following handout: Handout-1-Vietnam-War-Document-Based-Question.pdf (teachrock.wpenginepowered.com)

In addition, print slips of paper with major events from the time period the DBQ covers. For instance, the slips might include:

- The Gulf of Tonkin Incident
- The Geneva Accords
- Battle of Dien Bien Phu

- The 1968 Democratic National Convention
- The Tet Offensive
- Kent State Shootings
- Fall of Saigon
- The Pentagon Paper
- Operation Rolling Thunder
- US Withdrawal from Vietnam
- My Lai Massacre
- Any other important event your class studied during the Vietnam War period

Have learners work in small groups to arrange the primary sources provided in the handout and the events in a timeline. After groups have successfully completed the timeline, ask them to reflect (in writing) on the following questions:

- How did the Vietnam War progress through the 1950s, 1960s, and 1970s? Were there any major defeats or victories, for either side? Support your response with at least three pieces of evidence from your timelines.
- How did America's role in Vietnam change over the course of the war? Did musicians' views on the war change? Find examples from the documents that support your response.

Day 2

Split the class into four or five groups, and assign each group one or two documents from the Handout provided Day 1. Then distribute "The HIPPO technique for Analyzing Documents": Handout-2-The-HIPPO-Technique-for-Analyzing-Documents.pdf (teachrock.wpenginepowered.com)

Have the groups to analyze the document(s) assigned to them using the HIPPO process.

The assign just one document in handout one to each individual. Inform learners that they have eight minutes to analyze their assigned document. Learners should examine and research some or all of these elements of their document and to specifically address the following:

- Who created the document?
- When was it created? Was it created in response to any particular historical events?
- Does the author discuss any other issues present at the time, outside the Vietnam War?
- Where was it created? Is there any significance to that place?
- What is the content of the primary source? What is the author's main point? Is there anything surprising?

Next, explain to learners that they may write notes on their primary sources to help them remember the key points, but encourage them to become 'experts' on their documents. After the eight minutes have expired, it is time for the cocktail party. Learners will circulate amongst themselves in order to learn about the documents from one another. Explain the following ground rules:

- Meet in pairs only
- The person with the earliest birthday discusses his/her document first
- No talking to yourself… or someone who read the same document as you did

At the end of one minute, it is time to move on. (Project manager should monitor time and give a 30-second warning.) When learners have had the opportunity to meet with readers of all the other documents, have them return to their seats. Depending on the size of the class, you can have learners discuss as a whole or you can have them work in small groups. Either way, have learners respond to the following questions:

- How did intellectuals, writers, and musicians feel about the U.S.'s engagement with Vietnam? Were there differences in their opinions?
- Was there a significant change over time, as evidenced in the documents, in the reactions to the Vietnam War? Why do you think those changes occurred or failed to occur?

Day 3

Distribute to learners "Kent State Learners Killed by Troops": Handout-1-"4-Kent-State-Learners-Killed-by-Troops".pdf (teachrock.wpenginepowered.com)

Compel learners to clarify the "5 Ws" of this event:

- **What** is being discussed in this article?
- **Where** did the shootings occur?
- **When** did they occur?
- **Who** were the principal actors in this event?
- **Why** did the shootings occur?

Then play "Ohio" for learners: Ohio - TeachRock

Compel learners to respond to the following:

- What does the story of the song "Ohio" say about the effect the Vietnam War era had on musicians?
- In what ways do you think the song "Ohio" might have been a more effective method of expressing shock and opposition than any journalism could have been?
- Display for the class the lyrics to Ohio, which can be located via search engine, then have learners respond to the following:
- Who might Neil Young be referring to in the line "found her dead on the ground"?
- What do you think Neil Young means in the song with the lyric "we're finally on our own?"
- In what ways does this song represent an "in your face" protest? What is it calling into question?
- Do you think everyone agreed with Neil Young's view of what occurred at Kent State? Why do you think "Ohio" might have also been a "touchstone of opposition" for people that supported the Vietnam War?

Day 4

Inform learners that during much of the Vietnam War, Americans were split between groups known as the "Hawks," and the "Doves." Ask:

- Based on the label, what might have the "Doves" believed about the Vietnam War?
- What might have the "Hawks" believed about the Vietnam War?

Divide the class into five groups and distribute to each the following: Handout-2-Comparing-Hawks-and-Doves.pdf (teachrock.wpenginepowered.com)

Inform learners that they will be watching clips from *CNN's* "Soundtracks" and doing a Gallery Walk to examine more closely how the Hawks and Doves differed.

For each pair of images they see, learners must consider the following:

1. Compare the people seen in the images. Are there differences in the way the loo or act?
2. Based on the images, what sort of concerns do you think the Hawks and Doves emphasized? What motivated them to take the stance they took?
3. What might have been the differing values the Hawks and Doves embraced?
4. Who do you think represents "mainstream" American society, and who is pushing against it?
5. What else do you notice about these images that is similar or different?

The project manager is advised to place the Hawks and Doves Gallery Walk images around the classroom, and show the five Gallery Walk questions above. Have groups examine each image and make notes on their handout on the differences they see between the Hawks and Doves, using the questions displayed as a guide.

Then display the lyrics and play for learners "Okie From Muskogee": "Okie From Muskogee" - TeachRock

Have learners to respond to the following:

- The clip mentions that Nixon, in his election, made an appeal to the "Silent Majority." What kind of people might he have been referring to with this term? What sort of people was he NOT referring to?
- How might Merle Haggard's "Okie From Muskogee" also speak for "The Silent Majority"?
- Craig Werner describes the song as "Directed against the excesses of the Anti-war movement." Based on the lyrics, how does Merle Haggard describe such excesses? How does he characterize the anti-war movement?
- Do you agree with Craig Werner's assertion that the song was not a pro-war song, but an anti-anti-war song? Is there a difference between these two types of songs? Why or why not?

Play Edwin Starr's "War": "War" - TeachRock

Have learners to respond to the following:

- As Roger Steffens mentions, Richard Nixon campaigned for president on the promise to end the war in Vietnam. According to the clip, what happened instead? (*Nixon expanded the war by invading Cambodia*).
- According to the clip, was Kent State the only school in which the national guard shot learners? Where else were learners shot?

Display the two quotes below:

"The song was never about the Vietnam War. It was about the neighborhood wars and the racial wars that were going on inside America at the time. It just happened to coincide with the war in Vietnam."

"Why should they ask me to put on a uniform and go 10,000 miles from home and drop bombs and bullets on Brown people in Vietnam while so-called Negro people in Louisville are treated like dogs and denied simple human rights? No I'm not going 10,000 miles from home to help murder and burn another poor nation simply to continue the domination of white slave masters of the darker people the world over. This is the day when such evils must come to an end. I have been warned that to take such a stand would cost me millions of dollars. But I have said it once and I will say it again. The real enemy of my people is here. I will not disgrace my religion, my people or myself by becoming a tool to enslave those who are fighting for their own justice, freedom and equality. If I thought the war was going to bring freedom and equality to 22 million of my people, they wouldn't have to draft me, I'd join tomorrow. I have nothing to lose by standing up for my beliefs. So I'll go to jail, so what? We've been in jail for 400 years."

– Muhammad Ali

Have learners to respond to the following:

- What might Edwin Starr be referring to when he says "neighborhood and racial wars?"
- What might Muhammad Ali mean when he says "We've been in jail for four hundred years." Who is he referring to?
- Based on the quotes and the clip, how might the anti-war movement had particular relevance to African Americans? Are there any ways it might have been less relevant for them?
- Both Edwin Starr's "War" and Merle Haggard's "Okie From Muskogee" were not originally intended to be about the Vietnam War. What was it about the songs that led to their appropriation by the Hawks and Doves?

Day 5

Have the previously established groups review the notes they took comparing Hawks to Doves the previous day and to complete the following sentences:

- "The Doves opposed the Vietnam War because…"
- "The Hawks supported the Vietnam War because…"

Then have each group read their sentences out loud, and discuss the ways the statements between groups may be similar or different.

Then watch the full "Soundtracks" episode (42 minutes) on Kent State and the Vietnam War: Soundtracks episode 101 (cnn.com)

As an exit ticket, have each learner choose another song discussed in the episode and explain: Did the song represent the feelings of the Doves, Hawks, or neither? Explain.

Day 6

The project manager is advised to present the following information to learners:

Just as the United States has a long, complicated history of war and international conflict, so too has the nation seen resistance to that activity. During the 1960s, however, protest against war became a particularly visible part of American life. Television, a relatively new phenomenon, showed both graphic, often brutal images of the Vietnam War and footage of social and political unrest at home. In this particularly fraught moment in American history, protest music was among the most powerful means of voicing opposition to the US's involvement in the Vietnam War. Although protest music was not new — one finds rich examples of music calling for change in slave spirituals, labor songs, and even the popular songs produced on Tin Pan Alley during the first World War, for instance — it reached new heights in the 1960s, as many young Americans, facing mandatory participation in the war, grew increasingly outspoken in their dissent. Prior to the antiwar demonstrations on and around college campuses, the Civil Rights movement in particular had increased learner activism. As American involvement in Vietnam deepened, many in that age group faced the disconcerting reality of conscription. Even before they shipped out, those who were drafted had begun to see the horrors of the war, most notably on television. The growing presence of television in nearly every American household thus exacerbated divisions over the conflict and helped fuel the antiwar movement. What Americans watched on television each night shaped their perceptions of the Vietnam War, which came to be known as the "living room war." For some young Americans, called on to fight but unable to vote until the age of 21, the situation was unacceptable. Social protest provided young people with a voice they didn't always have at the ballot box. Popular music, already a vital part of youth culture by the mid-1960s, became a vehicle through which they could hear their concerns put to music. The music helped to build the antiwar community. In earlier eras, protest music sometimes had a subtle tone, propelled by acoustic instruments. By the late 1960s, however, it took on the instrumentation of Rock and Roll and made its way to the top of the charts. Not until 1971 did the 26th Amendment grant suffrage to 18-year-olds, empowering those most directly affected by the military draft. With the war increasingly unpopular at home and no American victory in sight, the United States negotiated a peace treaty and withdrew from Vietnam in 1975. The music of 1960s protest, however, remained among the era's most enduring legacies.

After presenting the information above, show learners the following two magazine covers:
World_War_I_and_Vietnam_Era_Magazine_Covers.jpg (632×417) (teachrock.wpenginepowered.com)

Direct learners' attention first to the cover of the *Saturday Evening Post* from February 22, 1919. Ask:

- What words come to mind to describe the soldier in this image?
- How do the children in the picture appear to feel about the soldier?
- What attitude toward war and soldiers does the picture convey?
- How do you imagine young Americans would have responded to the first image in 1919?

Then have learners examine the second image, the cover of *LIFE* from February 11, 1966. Ask:

- What words come to mind to describe the soldiers in this image?
- What attitude toward war and soldiers does this picture convey?
- How do you imagine a young person in 1966 would have responded to this image?

Then have learners compare the two images:

- What kind of picture is shown on each cover? (The first is an illustration, the second a photograph.) Explain to learners that the first image was created by Norman Rockwell, an illustrator known for his often-sentimental images of everyday life in America.
- Which war is depicted in each magazine cover? (World War I and the Vietnam War.)
- What overall conclusions can you draw about changes in the way war was represented to Americans by the media between World War I and the Vietnam conflict?

Lastly, show the following image of a man and woman (presumably husband and wife) watching footage of the Vietnam War in their living room:
Man_and_woman_watching_footage_of_Vietnam_War_LOC.jpg (640×413)
(teachrock.wpenginepowered.com)

Then read aloud the following quote from *The "Uncensored War": The Media and Vietnam*, by Daniel C. Hallin:

"Television news came of age on the eve of Vietnam. The *CBS* and *NBC* evening news broadcasts took their present form in September, 1963, expanding from fifteen minutes to half an hour…. The first exclusive stories the expanded shows were able to broadcast had to do with Vietnam…. Two years later, American troops went to war under the glare of the television spotlight. Vietnam was America's first true televised war."

Next, display for learners two graphs showing the growing number of television households in the United States and briefly discuss: Television_Households_in_the_United_States.png (712×852) (teachrock.wpenginepowered.com)

Compel learners to respond to the following:

- During which five-year period did television ownership in the United States grow the fastest? How does this growth appear on the line chart?
- In which decade did the number of households with televisions surpass 90 percent?
- What conclusions can you draw from these statistics about how much access to television news programming Americans had in 1950? In 1970?

Day 7

Explain to learners that they are about to see a series of unedited content taped for potential use in news broadcasts related to the Vietnam War. This footage was shot in 1969 and provides a "behind the scenes" look into what news reporters were seeing when they covered the war and what networks were gathering. Explain to learners that American men between the ages of 18 and 26 were required by U.S. law to register with the Selective Service System. Every registrant was assigned a selective service number. In December 1969, two lotteries were held. These lotteries determined the order in which men born from 1944 through 1950 were required to report for military service in the year 1970. Learners should know that this process is typically referred to as the "draft." Until the 26th Amendment to the U.S. Constitution was adopted in July of 1971, the voting age was 21. Therefore, many of the young men being drafted into the military could not vote, which meant they could not vote the politicians making decisions about the Vietnam War in or out of office. They did not have a say in the political process.

Play for the class footage from Vietnam: Vietnam Era News Footage - TeachRock

Then ask learners to imagine that it is 1970, and they are 18 years old and respond to the following:

- How would they feel if they, their family members, or their friends were required to fight in the war in Vietnam? How might seeing the war on television make you feel about this?
- Next, have learners imagine that they are going to write or listen to some music to express their feelings about the war. What would the lyrics be about? What might the music sound like?

As a class, listen to and analyze clips of two Vietnam War-era protest songs, Edwin Starr's "War" and "Ohio" by Crosby, Stills, Nash, and Young.

Play "War": "War" - TeachRock

Have learners respond to the following:

- What is the song about? What message do the lyrics send?
- How would you describe the style of the music?
- What instruments do you hear? (Drums, bass, tambourine, electric guitar, saxophone.)
- What adjectives would you use to describe the sound of the music? Does the sound of the music complement the meaning of the lyrics?

Explain that this song was released in 1970, the same year the first soldiers selected in the draft lottery were sent overseas. Ask:

- Do you think a song like Edwin Starr's would have been popular or unpopular in that year?

Display for learners the chart showing the top five songs in Billboard's popularity chart for September 5, 1970: Billboard_Hot_100_Sept_5_1970_.png (1036×470) (teachrock.wpenginepowered.com)

Ask:

- What position does "War" hold?
- How many weeks has it been on the popularity chart? What date did it first chart?
- What conclusions can you draw about how popular this song was in 1970? Why do you think it was so popular?

Play "Ohio" and have learners read the lyrics, which can be located via search engine: "Ohio" - TeachRock

Explain to learners that the song is about an antiwar protest at Kent State University in Ohio on May 4, 1970. Young people were holding rallies to protest a decision made by President Richard Nixon to bomb the country of Cambodia (which is next to Vietnam), thereby expanding the war in Southeast Asia. The Ohio National Guard was called in to control the protests. The Guard fired bullets into a crowd of learner protestors, killing four and injuring nine.

Play video of Graham Nash discussing the song and briefly discuss: Graham Nash on "Ohio" - TeachRock

Have learners respond to the following:

- What was the process by which Crosby, Stills, Nash and Young wrote and recorded "Ohio"?
- Why did they scrap their top-selling single to record a protest song?
- What does this process, and the speed with which they executed and distributed the recording, tell us about protest music's relevance and potential impact?

Ask learners to revisit their answers to the discussion questions, then have the class respond to the following:

- Did the songs "War" and "Ohio" sound like the music they thought they would have wanted to hear as teenagers in 1970? Why or why not?

Day 8

Distribute to learners an analysis chart: Microsoft Word - Handout 1 - Antiwar Protest Music.edited.doc (teachrock.wpenginepowered.com)

Then play Phil Ochs' "I Ain't Marching Any More:" Phil Ochs - I Ain't Marchin' Anymore / with lyrics - YouTube

Compel learners to fill in the portion of the chart pertaining to "I Ain't Marching Any More."

Then play John Lennon's "Give Peace a Chance:" Give Peace A Chance - John Lennon - Official Lyrics - YouTube

Have learners fill in the portion of the chart pertaining to "Give Peach a Chance."

Play Country Joe and the Fish's "I Feel Like I'm Fixin' to Die Rag": Country Joe Mcdonald - Feel Like i'm Fixing to Die Rag - Woodstock '69 (youtube.com)

Have learners to fill in the portion of the chart pertaining to "I Feel Like I'm Fixin' to Die Rag."

Have learners watch Anti-Vietnam War protests from 1969, which are taken from unedited, behind-the-scenes footage: Anti-Vietnam War Protests - TeachRock

Have learners write a short description of what appears to be going on in each segment of the video and to note when and how music is used by the protestors. The project manager is advised to collect this as an exit ticket.

Day 9

The project manager is advised to start the period by playing for the class recordings of two popular songs from the World War I era.

Play "I Didn't Raise My Boy to Be a Soldier" (1915): I Didn't Raise My Boy to Be a Soldier - TeachRock

Play "Over There" (1917): Over There - TeachRock

Compel learners to write out their response to the following:

- How do the two songs present contrasting views toward the war?
- Which is more like the *Saturday Evening Post* cover in the motivational activity? Which has more in common with the protest songs of the 1960s?

- Next, have learners imagine they are an 18-year-old involved in the antiwar movement, and are about to be drafted. Write a letter to a friend that addresses the following:
- The impact of the media in shaping your perceptions of the war.
- How antiwar music both reflected and helped you express your feelings about the war.
- The impact of the 26th Amendment on your life.

This letter must be posted to the Google Class stream by 11:59 pm tonight.

Day 10

The project manager is advised to present the following information to learners:

According to the United States Department of Veterans Affairs, between 1964 and 1973, nearly nine million Americans served in the U.S. Armed Forces during the Vietnam War. About 3.5 million men and women were deployed to Southeast Asia where hostilities took place. 58,200 American armed service members died while serving in the war, and of those, 40,934 are classified as "Killed in Action," with an additional several thousand dying from wounds and illness during the time of the war. Many of those who survived their service in Southeast Asia and returned home to the U.S. were traumatized by the experience in a variety of ways. Today, it is estimated that 400 American Vietnam War veterans die each day. The Vietnam War reflected, and in many ways defined, one of the most turbulent time periods in U.S. history. The war caused deep divisions within American society. The split was often represented as a binary conflict between anti-war and pro-war citizens at home, characterized respectively as "doves" and "hawks." The public discord and voices within those movements was covered extensively by the U.S. media at home. However, the feelings and opinions American service members overseas had towards the war, either of protest, approval, or somewhere in between, were often muted or unheard. Soon popular music provided a voice for soldiers and other service men and women, and a message that expressed how they felt. During the Vietnam War, popular songs provided a cultural connection for those serving overseas to what was being heard back home in the U.S., and certain songs represented the messages and movements of the "doves" and "hawks." The popularity of these tunes in and around the battlefield in Vietnam allowed the voice and experience of armed service personnel to be amplified and illuminated. Whether it was the patriotic anthem, "The Ballad of the Green Berets," by Staff Sergeant Barry Sadler, or the disillusioned plea of "We Gotta Get Out of This Place" by the Animals, songs evoked a variety of emotions and opinions. In the years since the war ended, songs like Bruce Springsteen's "Born in the U.S.A." have sought to reflect the complicated experience of the Vietnam War veteran after they returned home. Decades now removed from this era, select songs are considered a cultural component of that time period. As a powerful soundtrack, the songs inform the story of how the nation, and in particular the veteran, experienced the war, and its aftermath.

After presenting the information above, show learners the rubric (see Day 15). Then distribute to learners "I Served in Vietnam, Here's My Soundtrack": Handout-"I-Served-in-Vietnam.-Here's-My-Soundtrack".pdf (teachrock.wpenginepowered.com)

Have learners read the article aloud as a class. Then ask learners to clarify the "5Ws":

- **What** is the document?
- **Who** wrote the article?
- **When** was the article published in *The New York Times*?
- **Why** was it published?
- **Where** did the information come from?

Conduct a Think, Pair, Square, Share activity. Arrange learners in pairs, and instruct them to discuss the article and take notes. Then, pair one group of learners with another, creating groups of four. Ask each pair within that group to share what they discussed while the other takes notes. Then, have the group of four develop a presentation for the rest of the class.

Distribute to learners: Handout-Song-Lyric-Analysis.pdf (teachrock.wpenginepowered.com)

Then play "The Ballad of the Green Berets": "The Ballad of the Green Berets" - TeachRock

Instruct pairs to complete the lyric analysis for the song by filling out Part 2 on page 1 of the handout. Have each pair share their analysis with the whole class.

Once completed, ask each individual to jot down their thoughts and ideas as they pertain to the following questions:

- How might people supportive of U.S. military involvement in the Vietnam War interpret this song? What about people opposed to the war?
- The pro-war side used this song to bolster their efforts to attract more people to enlist in the U.S. Armed Forces. What about this song and its lyrics might encourage people to enlist?
- How might you react to this song if you volunteered to enlist for military service in the war?
- How might you react to this song if you were subject to being drafted for military service in the war?
- Can you guess the percentage of people that volunteered to serve in the military during the Vietnam War?

Day 11

Distribute to learners "For Protecting Their Right, to Say Things That Are Wrong": Handout-"For-protecting-their-right-to-say-things-that-are-wrong.".pdf (teachrock.wpenginepowered.com)

Have learners read the article and then respond to the following:

- What is the author's point of view in this article?
- Who is the intended audience?
- How does this handout relate to the lyrics and message of "The Ballad of the Green Berets"?

Next, play for learners "These Boots Are Made For Walkin'": "These Boots Are Made for Walkin'" - TeachRock

Have learners address the following:

- Are you familiar with this song? If so, how are you familiar with it?
- How would you describe the song to someone?
- Why might the song have been popular with those serving in the military during the Vietnam War?
- How did Nancy Sinatra's attitude about the war evolve as a result of her visits?
- Can you support the troops while protesting the war? In what ways?
- How did the resulting tension between Nancy and her father, Frank Sinatra, a major celebrity for the older generation, reflect the generational divide in the country?

- How might a hit song contribute to and nurture a common experience shared by service people overseas and civilians at home?

Distribute to learners "A Letter to My Wife": Handout-"A-Letter-to-My-Wife".pdf (teachrock.wpenginepowered.com)

Have learners read the letter and respond to the following:

- How can a personal correspondence provide insight into an experience?
- Why might writing letters home be important to someone serving in the military overseas?
- What details about the author's experience in Vietnam are discussed?
- How does the author feel about his experience?

Distribute to learners "The Meatgrinder" Handout-"The-Meatgrinder".pdf (teachrock.wpenginepowered.com)

After reading, have learners respond to the following:

- What was the author's purpose of writing this reflection?
- What details about the author's experience in Vietnam are discussed?
- How does the author feel about his experience?
- How might this account of the horrors of war build personal empathy for all of those involved?

Day 13

Play for learners "We Gotta Get Out of This Place": "We Gotta Get Out of This Place" - TeachRock

Then have learners respond to the following:

- What specific lyrics in the song may have contributed to it becoming a universally acknowledged anthem for many U.S. military personnel serving in Vietnam during the war?
- Comparing the experiences described in "The Meatgrinder" to this song's main message, how do they inform and affect your opinions, attitudes, and feelings about war?

Play "Music and Black Servicemen": "Music and Black Servicemen" - TeachRock

Then have learners respond to the following:

- What particular difficulties did these servicemen experience when trying to listen to the music they preferred in Vietnam? Would you say their "Soundtrack" to the war was censored?
- In what ways did the racism common in the U.S. affect Black service members in Vietnam? What specific examples did those interviewed give?
- How did military leadership respond to their demands to be able to listen to Soul music?
- In what ways might the fight over music in Vietnam represent greater issues of racism and discrimination that affected Black service members and civilians?
- James Brown performed for U.S. troops in June 1968, shortly after the assassination of Dr. Martin Luther King, Jr. In 1968, Brown released his hit single "Say It Loud, I'm Black and I'm Proud". In the context of this video, how do you imagine he was received by service members?

Play "Born in the U.S.A": "Born In the U.S.A." - TeachRock

Next, have learners retrieve the "Song Lyrics Analysis" handout: Handout-Song-Lyric-Analysis.pdf (teachrock.wpenginepowered.com)

Instruct learners to reconvene as pairs to complete the lyric analysis for "Born in the U.S.A" by filling out Part 2 on page 3 of the handout. Have each pair share their analysis with the whole class.

Distribute to learners "The Bitter Homecoming": Handout-"The-Bitter-Homecoming".pdf (teachrock.wpenginepowered.com)

After reading the article, have learners respond to the following:

- How does this handout relate to the lyrics and message of "Born in the U.S.A." and all of the songs heard?
- How might you describe the veteran's experience after returning home from the Vietnam War?
- What happened during the Vietnam veteran's reunion in Washington, D.C.?
- How did the reunion affect the author?
- Did the event provide any resolution to the author's experience of serving in the Vietnam War?

Day 14

Show learners the rubric (Day 15) that will be used to evaluate their performance. Core standards compel learners into timed-writing activities. Here is the assignment: learners are to imagine it is 1969 and they are 18 years old and are confronting being drafted to fight in Vietnam. They are to write a letter to their congressman expressing their thoughts and ideas on the matter.

- The letter must be addressed to the learner's actual congress-person (in 1969).
- The letter must address whether the person believes the war is justified and explain why or why not.
- The letter writer must explain whether they are a "Hawk" or Dove" and explain what those two things mean and elaborate why they are hawk or dove.
- The learners must address whether they think it is fair that they can be drafted even though they can't vote until age 21 and explain their thinking on the matter.
- The learner must encourage the congressperson to listen to a song (pro or anti-war) on the matter that resonates with them and explain why it resonates with them.
- The letter must conclude with a reiteration of the main point.

Writing assignment is due in the Google Class stream by 11:59 pm tonight.

Day 15

Learners are to provide at least one peer review according to the following criteria:

Rubric

The peer reviewed here submitted their essay to the Google Class stream by 11:59 pm of Day 14. **(0-20 points)**

The peer's essay was free of spelling and grammar errors. **(0-10 points)**

The letter addressed to the learner's actual congress-person (in 1969). **(0-10 points)**

The letter addressed whether the person believed the war was justified and explained why or why not. **(0-20 points)**

The letter writer explained whether they were a "Hawk" or Dove" and explained what those two things mean and elaborated why they are hawk or dove. **(0-30 points)**

The essay addressed whether the essayist believed it was fair that they could be drafted even though they can't vote until age 21 and explained their thinking on the matter. **(0-20 points)**

The essayist reviewed here encouraged their congressperson to listen to a song (pro or anti-war) on the matter and explained why it resonated with them. **(0-20 points)**

The letter concludes with a reiteration of the main point of the letter. **(0-10 points)**

Total score _____

Project 14

"From Second to Third Wave Feminism"

Overview: In this project, learners will investigate second-wave feminism and the fight for women's liberation in the United States. Learners will analyze the work of author Betty Friedan and singer Lesley Gore and their influence on women of the 1960s and 70s. Learners will learn about female singer-songwriters who emerged from this moment in American history. Learners will also identify the origins of Third-Wave Feminism and explore the diversity of the movement's demands, attitudes, and tactics by immersing themselves in three musical cultures from the 1990s: the Riot Grrrl punk rock scene exemplified by the band Bikini Kill, the female-fronted hip hop scene exemplified by Salt-N-Pepa, and the Tejano music exemplified by Selena.

Objectives: By the conclusion of this project, learners will know the founding of Second-Wave Feminism and its guiding principles. Learners will know of Betty Friedan's book *The Feminine Mystique* and the impact it had in the United States in the 1960s. Learners will know about the Miss America protest in 1968. Learners will know the role music played in articulating the principles of the feminist movement. Learners will also be able to identify the principles and actions of the Second-Wave Feminist Movement by reading excerpts of Betty Friedan's *The Feminine Mystique,* watching clips from the *CNN* "Soundtracks" series, and analyzing the song "You Don't Own Me" by Lesley Gore. Upon completion of this project learners will know the important musical contributions of female Singer-Songwriters of the early 1970s, including Joni Mitchell, Carole King, and Janis Ian. Learners will know the historical context from which this music emerged, focusing on the burgeoning women's movement that challenged traditional roles of women in American society. Learners will be able to identify connections between artistic expression and the broader social context in which the expression occurs. Learners will be able to compare and contrast musical performances by women in different eras. Learners will be able to evaluate the degree to which key Singer-Songwriters gave voice to female empowerment in the early 1970s. Learners will analyze and interpret song lyrics, both in text and in performance, and present their findings to the class. Learners will compare the meanings and use of the terms "girl" and "woman" and relate them to the changing role of women. Learners will take a position on the role of the Singer-Songwriter in the Feminist Movement. By the end of the project, learners will know about the Anita Hill testimony, and its continued significance in American cultural politics. Learners will know about the development, goals, and tactics of Third-Wave Feminism in the early 1990s. Learners will know how the music of Bikini Kill, Salt-N-Pepa, and Selena reflected the Women's Rights issues characteristic of Third-Wave Feminism. Learners will also be able to trace Third-Wave Feminism's goals, ideals, and attitudes by examining the work of female musicians in three musical scenes in the 1990s: Riot Grrrl, Hip Hop, and Tejano music.

Essential Questions: What was Second-Wave Feminism, and how did music contribute to the movement? What did the success of the female Singer-Songwriters of the early 1970s reveal about the changing roles of women in the United States? What was Third Wave Feminism, why did it occur, and how did musicians address some of the movement's demands?

Grade: High School and University

Subject: History, Social Studies, ELA, General Music

Estimated Time: 15 class sessions (45 – 50-minute classes)

Day 1

The project manager is advised to begin the project by presenting the following information to the class:

With men beginning to return home from the battlefields of World War II in 1945, many Americans were eager for a sense of normalcy. Post-war economic growth, a booming birth rate, and the development of suburban living appealed to many young families as the nation moved into the 1950s. But suburban life relied heavily on gender expectations and the idea of the nuclear family: where men were expected to be the breadwinner and provider, with women left at home to tend to the kids and all of the household duties such as cooking and cleaning. This expectation of domesticity was reflected in pop culture, as well as the emerging consumer culture that targeted suburbanites with items like new household appliances. While the suburban lifestyle became part of the definition of the "American Dream," for many women who were seen as nothing but a housewife it was anything but a dream. One housewife who had begun to question this "problem that had no name" was Betty Friedan. Influenced by French feminist Simone de Beauvoir and her 1949 book, *The Second Sex,* Friedan published her own work titled *The Feminine Mystique*, in 1963. The book centered on how unhappy American housewives were, and the need for women to be more than just a housewife and mother. *The Feminine Mystique* was a hit as much as it was controversial, with many accusing Friedan of attempting to destroy the American family and demonizing happy housewives. In spite of the backlash, the book went on to sell about one million copies in its first year and influence a generation of women determined to carve out paths for themselves beyond societal expectations and pressures. The 1960s and 1970s saw women like Friedan becoming more vocal against societal norms that expected them to be obedient and domestic. One major event where this became apparent was the protest of the 1968 Miss America pageant in Atlantic City, New Jersey. Over 200 women participated in the demonstration, carrying signs and banners criticizing the pageant's focus on women's bodies and beauty ideals. The protest helped launch the women's liberation movement into the public as it was covered by several media outlets. A few years prior to the demonstration, seventeen-year-old singer Lesley Gore recorded the song "You Don't Own Me" in 1963. In the song, Gore emphasizes being independent and free to make choices as a young woman. It reached No. 2 on the *Billboard* Hot 100 in February 1964. While not intentionally written with the emerging feminists radicalized by Friedan's work in mind, "You Don't Own Me" soon became an unofficial anthem associated with Second-Wave Feminism. Second-Wave Feminism didn't only encourage women to aspire to break free from societal expectations for women and gender norms. It also mobilized women to fight for legislation that protected women and secured autonomy. For example, Title VII of the Civil Rights Act of 1964 outlawed discrimination based on sex. The U.S. Supreme Court decision in *Roe v. Wade* (1973) ruled that "unduly restrictive" state regulations on abortion are unconstitutional. Organizations also formed, such as the National Organization for Women (NOW) in 1964, whose first president was none other than Betty Friedan. Second-Wave Feminism continued the work of first wave feminists, who were victorious in their fight for women's suffrage in the early twentieth century. It also laid the foundation for Third-Wave Feminists of the early 1990s who centered their work around diversity and sexuality.

After presenting the information above, the project manager is advised to provide to learners several minutes to write down on a piece of paper what they think of when they hear the word "feminism." Tell learners they can make any association they would like to with the word, whether it's a person, place, object, feeling, time period, phrase, movies, music, books, etc.

After the time allotted, encourage learners to share what they wrote with the class. Together, create a class definition of the term "feminism."

Next, play a clip about Friedan and *The Feminine Mystique*, which can be located here: Betty Friedan and The Feminine Mystique - TeachRock

Have the class respond to the following:

- Based on the commentary from the people interviewed in the clip, what were traditional expectations of women?
- How did Betty Friedan's *The Feminine Mystique* attempt to challenge these traditional expectations?

Show learners the cover of the original print of *The Feminine Mystique* and distribute the following excerpt from *The Feminine Mystique*: The-Feminine-Mystique-Excerpt_Handout.pdf (teachrock.wpenginepowered.com)

Read the excerpt as a class. Then ask learners:

- According to the excerpt, what do you think is "the problem with no name"? Why would this problem have no name?
- What might Betty Friedan be claiming in *The Feminine Mystique*?
- Who do you think was Friedan's audience? What type or groups of women? Can you think of any groups of women excluded by Friedan's beliefs?
- Why do you think the book was controversial? How do you think it would be received if it were published today?

Play "A Cannon Shot" clip at the following web address: A Cannon Shot - TeachRock

Then ask learners:

- According to the clip, what are the connections between second-wave feminism and the generations of women prior?
- What are some events or earlier movements that may have inspired this generation of women to organize?
- Based on the video, list some of the topics mainstream second-wave feminists are questioning.

Play for learners the following clip from the 1968 Miss America Pageant Protests: The Miss America Pageant Protests - TeachRock

Ask learners:

- Why might have the Miss America Pageant been chosen as a place for this demonstration?
- This clip emphasizes how women organized together to protest the Miss America Pageant and the items that represented women's oppression. What do you think makes an effective protest?
- What might the "freedom trash can" symbolize? What other items aside from the bra shown, do you think women might have thrown in the freedom trash can?

Show learners Lesley Gore's "You Don't Own Me," which can be located here: "You Don't Own Me" - TeachRock

After watching, display the lyrics to the song, which can be located via search engine.

Ask learners:

- What do you think Gore is singing about?

- Gore was 17 at the time of recording "You Don't Own Me." Why might this have appealed to teenage girls and young women at the time?
- Why might the song have become associated with second-wave feminism and the Women's Liberation Movement? How do the messages of the song and the movement compare or relate?
- How should we define Second-Wave Feminism?
- What are some key issues they were fighting for?
- How does it relate to today's discourse around gender equality and gender overall?

Day 2

The project manager is advised to present the following to the class:

By the early 1970s, many young, middle-class women who were born during the Baby Boom, nurtured in the economic growth of the post-World War II era, and came of age during the tumultuous decade of the 1960s increasingly sought liberation from the traditional roles women were expected to play in postwar American society. These women increasingly wanted a greater voice both within and outside the home. They sought entrée into decidedly male-dominated professions such as advertising and journalism and advocated for greater control of their own bodies. The emergence of a successful group of female Singer-Songwriters in the early 1970s – Joni Mitchell, Carole King, Carly Simon, Janis Ian – both reflected and advanced this growing spirit of female empowerment. Yes, women had always played a role in American popular music, from Folk artists Joan Baez and Mary Travers (of Peter, Paul and Mary) to Jazz vocalists Sarah Vaughan and Ella Fitzgerald to the "Girl Groups" of the early 1960s. Composers and lyricists such as Ellie Greenwich and Cynthia Weil had worked behind the scenes writing songs that propelled other artists to stardom. But the new female Singer-Songwriters were different: they typically sang songs that they themselves had written, often autobiographical in character. They frequently performed them with their own piano or guitar accompaniment. And because of these factors, there was an increased sense of intimacy to the performances. Different from many earlier female vocalists, the Singer-Songwriters typically pushed for a heightened feeling of honesty and authenticity that meshed perfectly with the kinds of songs they were writing and singing. Many of the Singer-Songwriters' songs focused, as earlier Rock and Roll songs had, on themes of romance and heartbreak. But the perspective now was that of a different femininity. In some cases, this new breed of Singer-Songwriter told of experiences only a woman could have. In Joni Mitchell's cryptic "Little Green," from the critically acclaimed album *Blue*, she captured the sorrow of a young, unwed mother who feels compelled to give her child up for adoption. In "At Seventeen," Janis Ian conveys a young girl's pain at being deemed an "ugly duckling," challenging prevailing societal conventions of feminine beauty. As feminist activists such as Gloria Steinem called for equal pay for women in the workplace and advocated for reproductive rights, the new female Singer-Songwriters demonstrated that they were the artistic equal to their male counterparts and could even surpass them in popularity. Joni Mitchell's album *Blue* achieved a level of critical and artistic success that few albums in history could claim. Carole King's 1971 album *Tapestry* became the most commercially successful album of her era, with its broad, personal appeal. Perhaps no one personified the change in women's roles in popular music more than King. Co-writing with her then-husband Gerry Goffin in the early 1960s, King was one of the most successful songwriters of her era. But it was not until 1971 that she began to take center stage as a performer. The vast commercial success of *Tapestry* and other subsequent albums proved that the American public was more than ready for the transition.

After the presenting to learners the info above, ask them to respond to the following:

- What is the difference between calling someone a "girl" and calling her a "woman"?
- Why might someone refer to a grown woman as a girl? What does that imply?

- Do the females in the class think of themselves as girls or women? Why?

Then distribute to or display for learners the lyrics to "My Guy," written by Smokey Robinson: Microsoft Word - My Guy Lyrics.edited.doc (teachrock.org)

Then play for learners a clip of Mary Wells performing "My Guy" in 1965: My Guy - TeachRock

Ask learners to respond to the following:

- What is the song about? What kind of mood does it create?
- Explain to learners that "My Guy" was written by Smokey Robinson, who also co-wrote the Temptations' hit song "My Girl." Ask: Why do you think he titled the song "My Guy" and not "My Boy"? What does this suggest about attitudes toward women in this period?
- Do you think a man is qualified to write a song expressing a woman's feelings about her relationship with a man? Why or why not? Was something lost in an artistic way when women were not writing their own songs to sing?
- Look at the lyric "I'm sticking to my guy like a stamp to a letter." Overall, what does the song suggest about female roles? About what is worth singing about? About what is important in life?

Then explain to learners that "My Guy" was a No. 1 hit during the "Girl Group era" of the early to mid-1960s, when female vocal groups sang songs that were more frequently written by men than by women. Play the video clip of another hit from that era, the Shirelles performing "Will You Still Love Me Tomorrow" in 1964 (co-written by Carole King and her then-husband Gerry Goffin): Will You Still Love Me Tomorrow - TeachRock

Ask learners:

- What is the overall mood of the song? Is it similar to "My Guy?" In what ways? In what ways is it different?
- Play for learners the clip of King performing "Will You Still Lov Me Tomorrow," which was included on her 1971 masterpiece, *Tapestry*: Will You Still Love Me Tomorrow - TeachRock

Compel learners to compare the two versions of the song, specifically:

- Compare the performers' appearances. How are they dressed? What kind of facial expressions do they offer? What image of themselves are they presenting?
- What overall tone/mood does each version convey?
- Compare the vocal styles of each performance. How are voices used in each version?
- What are the performers in each video doing while singing? What message(s) do their actions convey?
- Would you classify the performers in each version as "girls" or "women"? Why?
- How is a song different when the person who wrote it performs it? Why might it be important to King to have recorded the song herself, even though it had already been a big hit?
- Based on what you have seen in these two performances, what do you think had changed in the United States between 1964 and 1971?

Day 3

Play for the class Joni Mitchell's "Woodstock" (1971), which can be located here: Woodstock - TeachRock

Play for the class Janis Ian's "At Seventeen" (1975): At Seventeen - TeachRock

Play for the class Carole King's "(You Make Me Feel Like a) Natural Woman" (1971): At Seventeen - TeachRock

Divide the class into three to six groups. Distribute to each group one of the following PDFs.

Handout 1: Microsoft Word - jonimitchellhandout.edited.doc (teachrock.wpenginepowered.com)

Handout 2: Microsoft Word - janisianhandout.edited.doc (teachrock.wpenginepowered.com)

Handout 3: Microsoft Word - carolekinghandout.edited.doc (teachrock.wpenginepowered.com)

Allow groups sufficient time to discuss the questions on the handout.

Have each group nominate a spokesperson who will report the group's general findings to the class as a whole. Presentations should include:

- The name of the artist and the song
- A brief summary of the subject of the song
- A brief summary of the musical style/sound of the song
- The group's analysis of what the artist is trying to say through the song
- The group's overall reaction to the song – what they liked about it (or didn't), what resonated with them, etc.

Discuss as a class:

- What do these songs have in common?
- What do you notice about these songs musically? Do they tend to have a strong beat?
- How does the singing style affect your reaction to the song?
- What about the themes of the songs? Are they happy and upbeat? What words would you use to describe them?
- How are they different from "My Guy"?
- Do these performers strike you as "girls" or "women"? How so?
- Could these songs have been written by men? Why or why not?
- The adage that "the personal is political" was frequently used during the feminist movement of the 1970s. Are these songs personal or political? Can they be both? Why do you think this phrase was used so often by feminists and others during this period?
- Do these songs have a special appeal for women? Or are they equally appealing to men? Should they be thought of as "women's songs," or just songs?
- Overall, do you think the music made by King and the other women in this lesson was political? Was it making a statement about changing roles of and attitudes toward women? Or was it just women making music that people wanted to listen to?

- What do you think women performing as Singer-Songwriters in this era contributed to popular music?

Day 4

Compel learners to think about music today and the styles it includes, the themes it addresses, and the performers who are most successful. Have learners respond to the following:

- How did the female Singer-Songwriters of the 1970s reflect changing attitudes toward women? Should their work be thought of as political, or were they just musicians making good music?

Play for learners the *ABC News Special*, "NOW: Women's Liberation" (1970): Now: Women's Liberation - TeachRock

Then compel learners to begin outlining a 300–500-word response to the special. The essayist must define feminism according to the definition established by the class (i.e. not just the dictionary version). The essayist must also describe/elaborate the ambitions of the women's movement in that time and place. The essayist must elaborate how the video connects what was happening at the time with female Singer-Songwriters explored during the course of this project. Learners must also compare the female Singer-Songwriters of the early 1970s to those popular today, such as Adele or Taylor Swift. In what ways is their work similar? In what ways is it different? Learners are tasked with considering the musical styles as well as the themes they address in their work. Learners must address whether or not these newer artists achieved popularity primarily with girls and women, or do they speak to a wider audience? The project manager is advised to apprise the class of the rubric that will be used to evaluate them (see Day 6).

Day 5

Introduce learners to the RADAR revision method and encourage the class to implement some of the strategies as they are revising. Provide learners the period to construct a written and revised response that significantly addresses the questions above. This assignment must be posted to the Google Class stream by 11:59 pm tonight.

Day 6

Learners will provide at least one peer review according to the following criteria:

Rubric-1

The essayist peer reviewed here posted their assignment to the Google Class stream by 11:59 pm of Day 5. **(0-20 points)**

The essayist defined feminism according to the definition established by the class (I.e. not just the dictionary version). **(0-20 points)**

The essayist peer reviewed here significantly described/elaborated the ambitions of the women's movement during the late-1960s – early 1980s. **(0-20 points)**

The essayist elaborated how the info in the video connected to what was happening at the time with female Singer-Songwriters explored during the course of this project. **(0-20 points)**

The essayist compared the female Singer-Songwriters of the early 1970s to those popular today, such as Adele or Taylor Swift, paying particular attention to the ways is their work similar and/or different. **(0-20 points)**

The essayist considered whether female musical artists of today have achieved popularity primarily with girls and women, or whether they speak to a wider audience. **(0-20 points)**

The essay was free of spelling errors and seem polished and professional grade. **(0-20 points)**

Total score _____

Day 7

The project manager is advised to present the following information to transition from Second Wave to Third-Wave Feminism:

In 1991, law professor Anita Hill appeared in front of the U.S. Senate Judiciary Committee on the confirmation of Judge Clarence Thomas to the Supreme Court. Before the committee, she testified that Thomas, her former boss, sexually harassed her in the workplace. The nationally televised hearings showed the harsh, humiliating, and dismissive treatment Hill—a black woman —received from a committee made up solely of white men. Judge Thomas was eventually confirmed to the Supreme Court, but the hearing reawakened a national discussion on sexual politics and the continued gender inequality in the United States. Reactions to Thomas' confirmation varied from elation to fury, especially amongst young women. The strong feelings that emerged from the Anita Hill case helped initiate the moment that is now referred to as "Third-Wave Feminism." Third-Wave Feminism was spearheaded by young, college-aged women, many of whom grew up with feminist mothers who fought for women's rights in the 1960s and 1970s. Feeling a growing need to draw awareness to unsolved issues, from sexual assault to equal pay, their form of activism was not like their mothers' generation. It was loud, raucous, and messy. Where Second-Wave Feminists tried to rally women around universal womanhood, Third Wavers recognized that feminism contained multitudes of intersections to address. Just as in Second-Wave Feminism, music became one of the primary ways to define and spread the demands of the Third Wave. Inspired by the Punk rock "Do-It-Yourself" (DIY) ethos, in the early 1990s, females in the Pacific Northwest picked up instruments and formed their own bands and scenes, refusing to let their music or their image be dictated by what men defined as good. Led by feminist artist Kathleen Hanna, Bikini Kill became the de facto head of the Riot Grrrl movement. With aggressively political topics, the band carved out a niche space in rock to reflect the ideals and concerns young feminists of the '90s were embracing. As political and well-intentioned as the feminism of Riot Grrrl was, however, it was criticized by some for centering primarily white and cisgender women. But other genres provided women of color with representations of empowerment and visibility. In Hip Hop, female rappers used their rhymes to speak about mistreatment by men, in and out of the industry, and to uplift women, especially black women. Rap trio Salt-N-Pepa found success with songs dedicated to openly talking about sex, gender roles, HIV/AIDS, and relationships. The proclaimed "First Ladies of Rap" even became the first female rap group to win the Grammy for Best Rap Performance by a Duo or Group. Meanwhile, Tejano music, a genre originating in Texas and rooted in Mexican-American culture, saw the rise of Selena Quintanilla-Pérez in the 1980s and into the 1990s. While it included several female musicians, Tejano was mostly a male dominated genre. But Selena was able to breakthrough and achieve success. She sang about love and relationships, but outside of music, Selena became a fashion icon due to her curve hugging outfits that bared her midriff. She also was an entrepreneur who launched a fashion line, opened boutiques, signed a contract with Coca-Cola to be their spokesperson and did philanthropy work.

After the presentation, the project manager is advised to apprise learners of any rubrics that will be used to evaluate them during the duration of the project. Next, have learners write on a scratch piece of paper a list of political, social, and cultural accomplishments they think women have made in the past 100 years. Then ask learners to write a separate list of issues women continue to face today. Ask learners to share their answers, and discuss what issues facing women they feel have been overcome, and which are still in progress. Then present the following image to the class: Anita Hill before Congress - TeachRock

Before identifying the event in the photograph, the project manager is advised to ask learners to take notes on what they notice (a black woman alone at a small table across from a large table comprised of white men in suits).

Have learners respond to the following:

- Where might the location of this photograph be?
- What is occurring in this photograph?
- For those who might not know what is captured in this photograph, what conclusions can you draw based on the context clues from your notes?
- Does anyone know what historic event is being captured according to this photograph?

Show The New York Times Explanation of Hill's Testimony, which can be located here: Anita Hill Hearing: An All-Male Panel With an Agenda - The New York Times (nytimes.com)

Have learners respond to the following:

- What was at issue in the Anita Hill hearings?
- Why was she brought to testify before senate?
- In what ways did some see the Anita Hill testimony as inherently unfair?
- What was the result of the Anita Hill hearings?

Display for the class "Thank You America (Anita Hill)" by Sue Coe (1991), which can be located here: Sue Coe, "Thank You America (Anita Hill, Study for the lithograph of the same title)" (1991) | PAFA - Pennsylvania Academy of the Fine Arts

Inform learners that the image is by British-American illustrator Sue Coe, who made the piece in response to the trial. Then ask learners:

- How is Anita Hill being portrayed in this image?
- What statement might Coe be making in portraying Hill in this way?
- How are the senators portrayed in the image?
- How is the media portrayed in the image?
- What else do you notice about this image?
- Based on what you learned in the video, how might this art piece represent the feelings some Americans had about the Anita Hill hearings?

Encourage learners to take notes while watching Harvard law learners responding to Anita Hill's testimony: Harvard Law Learners Respond to the Anita Hill Testimony - TeachRock

After the clip, ask learners:

- Which opinions in the clip did you find particularly interesting? Why?
- Was there an opinion you found yourself most in agreement with? Which opinions did you disagree with? Why did you feel this way about the opinion?
- What issues do the law learners bring up in this video that you feel still affect women today?
- Are there any issues the learners bring up that you feel is no longer pertinent today?

Day 8

Distribute to learners Rebecca Walker's "I Am the Third Wave," which can be located here: Handout-1-Rebecca-Walker-"I-Am-the-Third-Wave".pdf (teachrock.wpenginepowered.com)

Provide ample time for learners to read the article, highlighting and taking notes of what they find most interesting.

Then ask leaners to response to the following questions:

- How did the Anita Hill hearing affect the Walker? For her, what were the hearings about?
- For Walker, what message did Clarence Thomas's promotion to the Supreme Court send?
- What sort of issues do women continue to confront, according to this essay?
- The phrase "The personal is political" was commonly used during the "Second Wave" feminist movement in the 1960s and 70s. How does Rebecca Walker mix the personal with the political in this article?
- This article was first published in Ms. Magazine, which was a product of the second wave feminist movement in the 1960s and 1970s. What message do you think Walker is sending the readers of this magazine?
- Robin Morgan states that many women involved in Third Wave Feminism often had feminist mothers, but felt the accomplishments of past feminist movements were not "filtering into their lives," which made them "angry." Do you think Rebecca Walker's essay reflects this argument? Why or why not?

Distribute the following PDF, which delves into the Tejano genre and role of Selena in it: TejanoSelena-Document-Set.pdf (teachrock.wpenginepowered.com)

Play for learners Selena: Selena - Como La Flor (Live From Astrodome) - YouTube

Distribute the following PDF, which delves into the Hip Hop genre and the group Salt-N-Pepa: Hip-Hop-Document-Set.pdf (teachrock.org)

Play for learners Salt-N-Pepa: Hip Hop/Salt-N-Pepa - TeachRock

Distribute the following PDF, which delves into the Riot Grrrl genre and the band Bikini Kill: Riot-Grrrl-Document-Set-High-School.pdf (teachrock.wpenginepowered.com)

Play for learners Bikini Kill: Riot Grrrl/Bikini Kill - TeachRock

Day 9

Provide learners the first half of the class to review six primary sources provided and then begin to review the documents in search of evidence to answer the following questions:

- Can you think of any contemporary musicians who may have been inspired by any of the musicians discussed in class during the course of this project?
- Can you think of any contemporary musicians who address similar issues as Bikini Kill, Salt-N-Pepa, or Selena? If so, who and how?
- Do the issues articulated or characteristic in the careers of Bikini Kill, Salt-N-Pepa, and Selena persist today? If so, in what ways?
- Are there any additional issues current musicians are speaking out against that were not addressed by the three artists covered in class?
- Are the issues Third Wave Feminism spoke out against still prevalent today? If so, in which ways?

A hard copy of this is to be turned in to the project manager by the end of the period.

Day 10

The project manager is advised to present some examples of Zines to the class and explain what a Zine is and its potential purposes (politics, humor, etc).

Learners are to make a short three-to-four page 'zine that showcases their personality, the things they like, and the beliefs they stand for. Learners are also tasked with creating a playlist of 10 songs that exemplify some of the beliefs they identify with. The learners must add a blurb about each song explaining ho the song says something or delves into in some way the learners' belief system.

Day 11

Learners need to revise their tasks from Day 10 and begin to construct a presentation that contains that information.

Day 12

Learners need to put finishing touches on their presentations and solicit feedback from peers. Presentations must be posted to the Google Class stream by 11:59 pm tonight.

Day 13 and 14

Learners present. The project manager is advised to distribute rubrics for peer evaluation on the first day of presentations since they will need to evaluate a peer's performance in terms of presenting. The project manager should assign whom peer reviews whom before distributing evaluation forms to the class.

Day 15

Learners will provide at least one peer review according to the following criteria:

Rubric-2

The peer reviewed here posted their presentation to the Google Class stream by 11:59 pm of Day 12. **(0-20 points)**

The peer reviewed here kept their presentation between 3 – 4 minutes. **(0-10 points)**

The presentation included a short three-to-four page 'zine that showcased the peer's personality, the things they like, and the beliefs they stand for. **(0-30 points)**

The presentation included a playlist of ten songs that exemplify some of the beliefs the presenter identified with. **(0-20 points)**

The presentation included a blurb about each song on the playlist that in some way elaborated how that song meshed with the peer's beliefs. **(0-20 points)**

The presenter was ready, willing, and able to present when called upon. **(0-10 points)**

The presentation seemed rehearsed (i.e. not the first time it had been presented). **(0-10 points)**

The presentation was free of spelling and grammar errors. **(0-10 points)**

Total score _____

Project 15

"A Century of American Indian History in Music"

Overview: Learners are introduced to Pat Vegas and Redbone. Learners then look back to the late nineteenth century to consider the significance of Redbone's success. Learners will use clips from the film, as well as a set of seven source documents to assess the U.S. government's attempt to control Native American populations by way of culture, particularly music. The documents, which include letters, acts of Congress, testimony, and newspaper articles, introduce learners to legislation and the Federal Indian Boarding School system from the perspectives of both government agents and Native Americans. Additionally, learners will analyze three poems that speak to the trauma Native Americans have experienced due to such governmental policies.

Objectives: By the end of the project, learners will know the history of the Massacre at Wounded Knee from several perspectives, will know about the Dawes Act, will know about the Carlisle Indian Boarding School and Federal Indian schools of the late -nineteenth and early twentieth centuries. Learners will know firsthand accounts of learners' experiences at Federal Indian Schools. Learners will know about Colonel Richard Pratt and the movement to "civilize" Native Americans during the period. Learners will know about mainstream white feelings toward to the music culture of Native Americans. Learners will know about Pat and Lolly Vegas (Vasquez) and their band Redbone. Finally, through analysis of source documents, learners will be able to discuss how attitudes toward Native American culture impacted the events at Wounded Knee, and apply their historical perspective to interpret the success of Native American popular music later in the twentieth century.

Essential Question: In what ways did the music of Native Americans mark them as outsiders from the developing narratives of "American-ness" in the late nineteenth and early twentieth centuries, and how did the federal government attempt to use music as a tool to force assimilation?

Grade: High School and University

Subject: History, Social Studies, ELA, General Music

Estimated Time: 5 class sessions (45 – 50-minute classes)

Day 1

Project managers are advised to begin by presenting the class with the following information:

To a present-day listener with no additional context, Redbone's single "Come and Get Your Love" may just sound like a classic mid-70s Rock tune. The song, which many might recognize from the opening sequence of the film *Guardians of the Galaxy*, is marked by a tight and funky drumbeat, as were many in that post-James Brown and Sly and the Family Stone moment. Its harmony is punctuated by a punchy, dry bass line that contrast with lush, rather deep-in-the-mix string overdubs. The sparse, repeated lyrics are not what many would call "deep." "Come and Get Your Love," however, is in many ways a breakthrough track. When "Come and Get Your Love" broke the *Billboard* Top 5 singles in 1974, and when the track went "Gold" (it sold at least half a million copies), it marked the first time an outwardly Native American ensemble had reached such heights. Pat and Lolly Vegas, the Yaqui, Shoshone, and Mexican American brothers who founded Redbone in 1969, hadn't always been "outwardly" Native American in performance. In the early 1960s, the brothers began their professional careers playing "Surf" music in Los Angeles. They recognized that their family surname, "Vasquez," would mark them as Mexican-American and limit their potential. So, the Vegas brothers were born. However, as national attitudes toward identity and ethnicity began to evolve later in the decade, the Vegas brothers decided to take the advice of part-Cherokee friend Jimi Hendrix and, as Pat Vegas puts it, "do the Indian thing." Redbone performed in Native American clothing, and also worked traditional drum, dance, and song into performances, even on TV. Redbone's success came less than a century after the U.S. government banned traditional expressions of Native American song and dance, and eighty-four years after the Massacre at Wounded Knee, where U.S. forces murdered between two-and three-hundred Lakota men, women, and children, ostensibly because they refused to cease performing a pan-tribal ritual known as the "Ghost Dance."

After presenting the information above, apprise them of the rubric that will be used to evaluate them during the course of tis project (see Day 5). Then ask learners to the following:

- Can you think of any times music feels like more than entertainment to you? When it might say something about who you are?

Play Pat Vegas' "Do The Indian Thing": Do The Indian Thing - TeachRock

Explain to learners that Pat Vegas was a Yaqui, Shoshone, and Mexican American musician whose band Redbone became the first Native American group to have a Gold (more than half-a-million sold) record in 1974.

The have learners respond to the following:

- What do you think Jimi Hendrix meant when he told Pat Vegas to "do the Indian thing"? Why do you think Pat Vegas might have chosen to downplay or hide his heritage before Redbone?
- What do you think David Fricke might mean when he says, "ultimately, getting through is the best revenge?" In what ways did Redbone "get through"?

Have learners make a T-chart on which each side represents one of the Redbone performances (the "traditional" and the Rock and Roll) in Clip 1.

Play "Redbone Chant": Redbone Chant - TeachRock

Play "Come Get Your Love": Come and Get Your Love - TeachRock

Have learners record their answers to the following questions on the T-Chart for each performance, then discuss their answers as a class:

- What instruments are being used?
- How would you describe the singing?
- How would you describe the dancing?
- Do you notice any similarities between the two clips?

Show the class the "Ghost Dance": The Ghost Dance and Wounded Knee - TeachRock

Have learners respond to the following:

- Why do you think Native American music was seen as "dangerous" and a "threat" by U.S. officials?

- What power do you think they might have believed Native American music had? In this clip, John Trudell suggests that the government agents wished to completely erase Native American culture, so "of course they came after our music." Why do you think he feels so sure that controlling music was a way for the government to control the people?
- How do you think an event such as the Massacre at Wounded Knee might impact the practice of traditional song and dance among other tribes in what is today the United States?

Day 2

Learners will respond to a Document Based Question (DBQ) using seven source documents from the period of Wounded Knee. Distribute the sources.

Document 1: "Excerpts from Richard H. Pratt's "The Advantages of Mingling Indians with Whites": The Ghost Dance and Wounded Knee - TeachRock

Document 2: "Native American Learners Write Letters Home from Boarding School": Document-2-and-3.pdf (teachrock.wpenginepowered.com)

Document 3: "The Dawes Act": Document-4.pdf (teachrock.wpenginepowered.com)

Document 4: "Assorted Accounts on Wounded Knee": Handout-5.pdf (teachrock.wpenginepowered.com)

Give learners time to read and process the documents.

Before the end of the period, have learners respond to the following:

- To what extent did the U.S. government seek to use culture to control Native Americans in the late 19th century?
- Using examples from the documents, characterize the philosophical underpinnings of these measures, i.e., were they "for good," or callous, etc?
- In what ways do you think these measures contributed to the Massacre at Wounded Knee? Why?

Inform learners that the cruel and discriminatory policies that banned cultural and spiritual expressions of Native life and that removed Native Children from their tribal homes to send them to faraway boarding schools have resulted in deep trauma among Indigenous People in what is today the United States. Then distribute "Three Poems by Indigenous Writers": Handout-5-Three-Poems-by-Indigenous-Writers.pdf (teachrock.wpenginepowered.com)

Provide learners time to read the three poems. Then have learners address the following questions:

- What is similar about these three poems?
- Each poem offers a different perspective. What sort of character is speaking in each poem? What is their relationship with the Indian School?
- What imagery is used to describe indigenous culture in the three poems? What imagery is used to describe white "western" culture?
- How is repetition used in the poems? What effect might it have?
- In what ways might these three poems speak to how Native Americans experienced trauma in these Indian Schools?

- Considering what you know now about responses to Native American music in the United States, how would you assess the significance of the Redbone clip that began this lesson?
- Can you think of any other elements of culture that have moved from a marginal or forbidden position within society to one of acceptance?
- Can you think of anything that is currently marginal which you believe will someday be accepted?

Day 3

The project manager is advised to define the terms "civilize" and "Euro-centric" for the class and then explain that the seven documents included in this project (see Day 2) demonstrate a concerted effort on the part of the U.S. government to attempt to "civilize" Native Americans by forcing them to adopt a Euro-centric approach to all facets of life. In a short essay, learners are to use these documents to explore other facets of Native American life that the U.S. government attempted to change with legislation and intervention.

Give learners the remainder of the period to review the documents and their notes in an effort to locate evidence to address the ways in which the U.S. government attempted to change with legislation and intervention numerous facets of Native American life.

Day 4

Learners are to use the period addressing the ways in which the U.S. government attempted to change with legislation and intervention numerous facets of Native American life by crafting an essay. The project manager is advised to review the rubric with the class so that as much clarity as possible is provided. Encourage learners to use the rubric as a guide. The essay between is to be posted to the Google Class stream by 11:59 pm tonight.

Day 5

Learners are to provide at least one peer review according to the following criteria:

Rubric

The group's essay was submitted to the google class stream by 11:59 pm of Day 4. **(0-20 points)**

The peer's thesis statement was as follows: In the nineteenth century, there was a concerted effort on the part of the U.S. government to attempt to "civilize" Native Americans by forcing them to adopt a Euro-centric approach to all facets of life.

The peer then defined "civilize" and "Euro-centric." **(0-20 points)**

The peer concluded 1 by elaborating the structure of the essay (and that structure was followed). **(0-10 points)**

In Paragraph 2, the peer provided an example of a way the U.S. government attempted to change a facet of Native American Life. **(0-10 points)**

In Paragraph 2, the peer provided evidence from a source provided earlier in the project. **(0-10 points)**

In Paragraph 3, the peer provided another example of a way the U.S. government attempted to change a facet of Native American Life. **(0-10 points)**

In Paragraph 3, the peer provided evidence from another source provided earlier in the project. **(0-10 points)**

In Paragraph 4, the peer provided another example of a way the U.S. government attempted to change a facet of Native American Life. **(0-10 points)**

In Paragraph 4, the peer provided evidence from another source provided earlier in the project. **(0-10 points)**

In Paragraph 5, the peer restated of thesis: In the nineteenth century, there was a concerted effort on the part of the U.S. government to attempt to "civilize" Native Americans by forcing them to adopt a Euro-centric approach to all facets of life. **(0-10 points)**

In Paragraph 5, the peer highlighted main ideas/points made in paragraphs two through four. **(0-10 points)**

Total score _____

Project 16

"The United Farmer Worker's Make Weapons of Words"

Overview: In this project, learners will examine the lyrics and context surrounding Nikki Darling's poem, "A Street Called Dolores Huerta" and Alice Bag's song of the same name. Learners will throughout the course of this project use the work of these artists as a lens through which to consider the importance of the United Farm Workers movement and to discuss the legacy of Dolores Huerta, one of the movement's central figures.

Objectives: By the end of the project, learners will know the historical conditions that led to the United Farm Workers' struggle for labor rights. Learners will know the significance of the United Farm Workers movement as a historical event. Learners will know the role of women in the United Farm Workers movement and the role played by Dolores Huerta in particular. Learners will know how these historical events and figures are recognized and remembered today. Learners will know the role music played in the United Farm Workers movement. Learners will be able to describe the ways in which the United Farm Workers movement and Dolores Huerta have contributed to contemporary Civil Rights issues and to the feminist movement by examining how poetry and music by Diana Garcia, Nikki Darling, and Alice Bag reflect the movement and its figures. Learners will also draw connections between the songs and poems and contemporary struggles for the recognition of marginalized groups.

Essential Question: Who is Dolores Huerta, what role did she play in the United Farm Workers movement, and how is she recognized today?

Grade: High School and University

Estimated Time: 5 class sessions (45 – 50-minute classes)

Subject: History, Social Studies, ELA, General Music

Day 1

The project manager is advised to present the information below:

Migrant labor has been essential for the agricultural industry in western states such as California, Oregon, Washington, Arizona, and New Mexico. In the twentieth century, Chinese, Japanese, Filipino, and Mexican immigrants performed much of the agricultural work in the western United States. The Bracero Program alone brought five million Mexican workers to the U.S. from 1942 to 1964 in an effort to solve labor shortages caused by World War II. Agricultural work was low-paid, physically demanding, and dangerous. The workers and their families lived in poverty and lacked educational opportunities. They faced violence and discrimination when they sought fair treatment and reasonable living conditions. Cesár Chávez (1927-1993) and Dolores Huerta (1930-) were the children of agricultural workers and were familiar with the challenges they faced. Chávez had even dropped out of school in the eighth grade in order to work to support his family. Both Chávez and Huerta were deeply committed to community organizing and fighting social and economic injustice. Together, in 1962 they launched the union that became known as the United Farm Workers to establish better pay and working conditions. The UFW understood that although the workers were very poor, they were able to wield significant power at the ballot box, through grassroots organization, and through boycotts. Over the course of the 1960s and 1970s, the UFW made great gains for workers' rights by establishing disability insurance for farmworkers, fighting the use of dangerous pesticides, raising wages, and eventually passing the Agricultural Labor Relations Act of 1975, which granted farmworkers the right to collectively organize. The farmworkers' movement became so influential that Miriam Powell called it "the civil rights movement of the West." One of the most successful boycotts was the National Boycott of California Table Grapes, which began as a Filipino workers' strike in 1965. To support the strike, the UFW organized a boycott of table grapes. Dolores Huerta's organizational skills were instrumental to this effort. She led picket lines and traveled to cities across the country to publicize the boycott and encourage the public not to buy grapes without union labels. The cause was boosted by the Civil Rights movement, which had increased public awareness regarding lowered standards of living for victims of racism and prejudice. Civil rights organizations, faith groups, learner activists, and even politicians such as Robert F. Kennedy brought attention to the UFW's cause. Soon, millions of consumers had joined the boycott and stopped buying table grapes. As a result, grape growers signed the first union contracts and brought social justice to agricultural labor. Yet while the United Farm Workers movement vastly improved working conditions, agricultural workers today still face low pay and high levels of discrimination and violence. They are still predominantly migrant workers and are often exploited by their employers, who ignore labor laws and fair practices. Dolores Huerta faced particular challenges as a woman in the predominantly male space of politics. For Huerta, fighting for gender equality was just as important as fighting for social and economic equality. Huerta fought gender discrimination within the UFW, where women were often constrained by the traditional views and gender expectations of their fathers or husbands. Huerta advocated for the participation of the entire family in the movement. After all, she argued, men, women, and children worked in the fields together. Following Huerta, women devoted their efforts to organizing at a grassroots level by joining the picket lines, organizing marches and boycotts, rallying for changes to legislation and policy, and registering Latinos to vote. Many of the tactics that the UFW pioneered have been adapted by other groups, from environmentalists to advocates for immigrants' rights. Huerta's slogan, *¡Si, se puede!* (Yes, we can!), was even adopted by President Barack Obama in his 2008 presidential campaign. Music, of course, played a central role in the grassroots efforts of the UFW. Songs provided a sense of community and connection for the movement, as the workers would sing at union meetings and as they marched or stood on the picket line. Some of the songs, such as "De Colores" or "Solidarity Forever," were traditional Spanish and American folk songs. Other songs, such as "El Picket Sign*,"* were written expressly for the movement by the Teatro Campesino, the cultural arm of the United Farm Workers. Music has also played a role in commemorating the movement and in recognizing Huerta's important contributions over sixty years of activism.

After the presentation, the project manager is advised to present any rubrics that will be used to evaluate learners' performance during the course of the project (see Day 5). Then, show any image of Delores Huerta to the class and ask if they recognize the woman in the photo. If nobody can connect the dots, inform them that she is Dolores Huerta, a civil rights activist who fights for workers' rights, women's rights, and Latinx rights.

Then distribute the following PDF: Handout-A-Street-Called-Dolores-Huerta-Nikki-Darling.pdf (teachrock.wpenginepowered.com)

Read the handout together and then ask learners to respond to the following:

- Why does the author think it is necessary to name a street after Dolores Huerta?
- The author imagines a street called Dolores Huerta. Why does the author think that this street would have potholes?

Show learners "A Street Called Delores Huerta, which can be found here": "A Street Called Dolores Huerta." - TeachRock

Have learners respond to the following:

- Compare Darling's poem with Alice Bag's performance. What changes did Alice Bag make?
- Does the music remind you of any other type of music you have heard or seen?
- Why do you think Dolores Huerta is inspirational for these artists?

Ask learners the following question and compile a master list:

- What is the name of the street the learner lives on?
- Are the streets in the learner's neighborhood or town named after a person?
- Are any schools in the area named after people? If so, who are they named after?

Again, the project manager is advised to compile a master list. This comes in handy on Day 4.

Day 2

To understand the historical context of the United Farm Workers (UFW), show learners part of the *PBS Series Latino Americans*: The Farm Worker Movement | PBS LearningMedia

Compel learners to respond to the following:

- Based on what you saw in the clip, what were the conditions like for farmworkers? Make a list of the hardships that they faced.
- Who was César Chávez?
- Who was Dolores Huerta?
- What is a union and why did Chávez and Huerta decide to form one? How might a union help the situation of the agricultural workers?
- What personal challenges did Huerta face?
- The UFW followed principles of non-violence in their protests and actions. Can you describe the actions that the United Farm Workers took to support and publicize the farmworkers' cause?
- What is a strike/*huelga*? Why did the workers strike?
- What symbols did the UFW use? Why did the UFW use Mexican and indigenous symbols and create signs and songs in Spanish? What did these symbols mean to the farmworkers?
- Describe the roles that Huerta and Chávez each took in the struggle for workers' rights. How do you think gender played a role in how Huerta was perceived and treated?
- What did the UFW achieve or gain with their actions such as the march to Sacramento? Explain how their movement and tactics might have led to these changes and accomplishments.

The project manager is advised to provide their own answers close to the end of the period so that the learners get a sense of the depth and specificity expected of them when analyzing media seen during projects.

Day 3

Distribute to learners "El Picket Sign" lyrics: Handout-"El-Picket-Sign"-Lyrics.pdf (teachrock.wpenginepowered.com)

Compel learners to respond to the following:

- What is being described in this song?
- What is this song advocating? Why might the song advocate that "the strike is good for everybody"?
- Based on what you've learned so far, who might "Pagarulo" and "The Zaninoviches" be? (Pagarulo and Zaninovich were prominent grape growers around Delano, California.)
- The lyrics refer to Benito Juárez, the first Indigenous President of Mexico, and Emiliano Zapata, who led a peasant revolution in Mexico in the early 20th century. What role do these figures play in the song? Why might have they been included?
- What role might have singing the song "El Picket Sign" played for workers striking or considering a strike?

Then distribute to learners "Huelga" by Diana Garcia: Handout-Huelga-Diana-García.pdf (teachrock.wpenginepowered.com)

Compel learners to read the handout. Then, ask them to draw a picture based on the description in the poem.

Display for learners Harvey Wilson Richards' iconic black and white photo of Delores Huerta hoisting a "Huelga" picket sign with the UFW eagle at top left of the sign, which can be located via search engine. Inform learners that the photograph displayed is the one that the poem describes. Ask learners to compare their drawing to the photograph. Then ask:

- How do the poem and the photograph portray Huerta? Make a list of her characteristics.

Lastly, give each learner the following transcript from a Huerta interview: Handout-Dolores-Huerta-Interview-Transcript.pdf (teachrock.wpenginepowered.com)

Have them respond to the following questions:

- Why does Huerta think that people don't want to get involved?
- According to Huerta, what is the difference between mobilizing and organizing? What examples does she give for each activity?
- Huerta argues that it is important for *everyone* to be involved. Who specifically does she mention in this interview? Can you think of other groups that should be included in politics and activism in your community?
- Why is it important for marginalized or underrepresented voices in the community to be heard? How can we give space and center marginalized people in movements?
- Why do you think it is important for working class people from marginalized groups and backgrounds to be represented and hold positions of power in politics, government, and in their communities?

Conclude by showing learners Huerta's Ted Talk, "Each Of Us Has A Voice, How Can We Use It For Social Change?: Dolores Huerta: Each Of Us Has A Voice, How Can We Use It For Social Change? : NPR

Day 4

Introduce learners to *ethos*, *pathos* and *logos* as rhetorical appeals. Then have learners write out the definition and give an example in their own words. Review the rubric with them (see Day 5). Then inform learners that Nikki Darling's poem and Alice Bag's performance from the Motivational Activity led to the inauguration of Dolores Huerta Square in East Los Angeles. Have learners respond to the following:

- Why are street names important?
- What can street names tell us about historical events or people?
- What is the relationship between a person and a street named after them?

Explain to learners that in many regions of the United States, streets are named for powerful figures who committed violent acts and were involved in atrocities such as slavery, white supremacy, or colonization. Ask learners to respond to the following:

- How might living on or near one of these streets feel for the marginalized communities that still bear the effects of these historical traumas?
- What should local governments do about this?

Use the master list of the street names you compiled with the class on Day 2.

- How many schools and/or streets are named after women?
- Are any ethnic names represented?
- For example, are there streets named for people of color, indigenous people, or immigrants?

Lastly, the learner is to think of someone – anyone – they admire. They are to write a letter to their local city council person (learners need to locate their council member and contact info) arguing why they think a street should be named after the person they choose. The learner is to employ *ethos*, *pathos* and *logos* when pitching their proposal to their city council person.

The letter should be structured as follows:

Add the city councilperson's name and email address before the letter.

Dear City Council Member XYZ,

I am writing to encourage you to name a street after (name of person and how you know this person – if you know this person – and why you believe they are worthy of having a street named after them in whatever town the learner is proposing a street be named after them).

Supporting paragraph 1: Learner must appeal to the councilmember's *ethos*.

Supporting paragraph 2: Learner must appeal to the councilmember's *pathos*.

Supporting paragraph 3: Learner must appeal to the councilmember's *logos*.

Concluding paragraph: Learner restates name of person and why the learner believes the person being nominated are worthy of having a street named after them in whatever town the learner is proposing a street be named after them.

A revised version of the letter must be submitted to the Google Class stream by 11:59 pm tonight.

Day 5

Learners will begin class by emailing their letter to their city councilperson. Learners will then provide at least once peer review according to the following criteria:

The peer reviewed here submitted their letter to the Google Class stream by 11:59 pm of Day 4. **(0-20 points)**

The peer review here provided the name and email of their city councilmember. **(0-10 points)**

The peer reviewed here began their letter with: Dear City Council Member (and added their name here) **(0-10 points)**

The opening paragraph was structured something like as follows: I am writing to encourage you to name a street after (name of person and how you know this person – if you know this person – and why you believe they are worthy of having a street named after them in whatever town the learner is proposing a street be named after them). **(0-20 points)**

Supporting paragraph 1 appealed to the councilmember's *ethos*. **(0-20 points)**

Supporting paragraph 2 appealed to councilmember's *pathos*. **(0-20 points)**

Supporting paragraph 3 appealed to the councilmember's *logos*. **(0-20 points)**

Concluding paragraph: Learner restated name of person and why the learner believes the person being nominated are worthy of having a street named after them in whatever town the learner is proposing a street be named after them. **(0-20 points)**

Total score _____

Project 17

"Reagan or the Deadhead's Cold War-era 'American Family'?"

Overview: Learners will examine ten primary source documents to consider the ways in which Ronald Reagan's policy decisions altered the trajectory of United States history. This project is based upon a Document-Based Question ("DBQ"), which is an assessment method commonly used in upper division and advanced placement courses. In a DBQ, learners are presented with 6-10 documents from varied sources, and are asked to synthesize the documents with their own knowledge to write a coherent thesis-driven essay. The goal of the activity is to challenge learners to think critically and to consider viewpoints that are frequently inconsistent and contradictory. Learners will also examine how the Deadhead lifestyle contrasts with the conservative version promoted by Reagan in the 1980s by analyzing clips from *Long Strange Trip* as well as historical documents, images, and videos.

Objectives: Upon completion of this project, learners will know Ronald Reagan's "Evil Empire" speech. Learners will know sting's "Russians," Steve Greenberg's "One Giant Step Backwards for Mankind," Reagan's "Tear Down this Wall" speech, Wasted Youth's "Reagan's In," and the Subhuman's "Human Error." Learners will be exposed to Francis Fukuyama's "The End of History?" Learners will also know Prince's "Ronnie, Talk to Russia." Learners will also evaluate how Americans responded to President Reagan's Cold War foreign policy agenda. By the end of the project, learners will know the Deadhead community and their subculture of fandom for the Grateful Dead. Learners will know President Ronald Reagan's historic election victory in 1980. Learners will know the similarities and differences between the Grateful Dead's Jerry Garcia and President Ronald Reagan. Learners will know President Ronald Reagan's particular set of promoted "family values" and consider whether those values can also be practiced by alternative communities like the Deadheads. Learners will also be able to compare the Deadhead lifestyle and culture with concurrent conservative American values promoted by President Ronald Reagan by examining footage from the film *Long Strange Trip* and historical artifacts.

Essential Questions: Did President Ronald Reagan's Cold War policies serve to heighten or to reduce tensions with the Soviet Union? Who are the Deadheads and how did their lifestyle contrast with the conservative values promoted by President Ronald Reagan in the 1980s?

Grade: High School and University

Subject: History, Social Studies, ELA, General Music

Estimated Time: 8 class sessions (45 – 50-minute classes)

Day 1

Distribute to learners "Reagan and the Cold War: A Document Based Question Activity: Handout-1-Cold-War-Document-Based-Question.pdf (teachrock.wpenginepowered.com)

In addition, print slips of paper with major events of the era. For instance, the slips might include:

- The Gulf of Tonkin Incident
- The Geneva Accords
- Battle of Dien Bien Phu
- The 1968 Democratic National Convention
- The Tet Offensive
- Kent State Shootings

- Fall of Saigon
- The Pentagon Papers
- Operation Rolling Thunder
- US Withdrawal from Vietnam
- My Lai Massacre
- Any other important event your class studied during the Cold War/Vietnam War period.

Next, have learners work in small groups to arrange the primary sources and the events in a timeline. After groups have successfully completed the timeline, ask them to reflect on these questions:

- How did the Vietnam War progress through the 1950s, 1960s, and 1970s? Were there any major defeats or victories, for either side? Support your response with at least three pieces of evidence from your timelines.
- How did America's role in Vietnam change over the course of the war?
- Did musicians' views on the war change? Find examples from the documents that support your response.

Assign each group a document or two embedded in Handout 1. Then distribute to each group a handout pertaining to the "HIPPO Technique for Analyzing Documents": Handout-2-The-HIPPO-Technique-for-Analyzing-Documents.pdf (teachrock.wpenginepowered.com)

Have groups analyze the document(s) assigned to them using the HIPPO process.

Have each group explain their document(s) to the class, based upon their HIPPO analysis.

Day 2

Cut out the documents and give each learner a single one. Apprise learners that they have eight minutes to analyze their assigned document. Learners should examine and research the following elements of their document:

- Who created it? (learners should are to be advised to research the authors' backgrounds)
- When was it created? Was it created in response to any particular historical events?
- Does the author discuss any other issues present at the time, outside the Vietnam War?
- Where was it created? Is there any significance to that place?
- What is the content of the primary source? What is the author's main point? Is there anything surprising?
- Learners may write notes on their primary sources to help them remember the key points, but encourage them to become 'experts' on their documents.

After the eight minutes have expired, it is time for the cocktail party. Learners will circulate amongst themselves in order to learn about the documents from one another. Explain the following ground rules:

- Meet in pairs only
- The person with the earliest birthday discusses his/her document first
- No talking to yourself . . . or someone who read the same document as you did

At the end of one minute, it is time to move on. The project manager is advised to monitor time and give a 30-second warning.

When learners have had the opportunity to meet with readers of all the other documents, have them return to their seats. Depending on the size of the class, the project manager can have learners discuss as a whole or can have them work in small groups. Either way, debrief and highlight the purpose of the activity have them respond to the following:

- How did intellectuals, writers, and musicians feel about the U.S.'s engagement with Vietnam? Were there differences in their opinions?
- Was there a significant change over time, as evidenced in the documents, in the reactions to the Vietnam War? Why do you think those changes occurred or failed to occur?

Day 3

The project manager is advised to begin the project by presenting the following information to learners:

During their thirty-year career releasing recordings and performing concerts around the world, the Grateful Dead established a legion of fans. Within this fanbase are the Deadheads, a unique group defined by their demonstrative passion for and connection to the band's recorded music and live performances – a devotion surpassing that of the casual Grateful Dead listener and concertgoer. For example, Deadheads often took to the road, indulging in a nomadic pilgrimage that found them following the band on tour and attending numerous shows per year. Over time, Deadheads became fixtures of the Grateful Dead concert experience, spawning a dynamic community that became omnipresent at each tour stop. Beyond their role in the Grateful Dead rolling roadshow, the wandering Deadhead community is often associated with ideals and traditions developed in the 1950s and 1960s counterculture movement – a whimsical outlook on life often defined by a rejection of established American social norms. Even in the 1980s, an era defined by the conservatism of President Ronald Reagan, the Grateful Dead saw a surge in popularity as a new generation of fans began to attend the band's shows and model the nomadic Deadhead journey. This uptick in the band's popularity provided a unique contrast between these two American cultural experiences. Reagan's landslide election victory in the 1980 United States presidential campaign represented a shift in American politics and society. A former governor of California, Reagan and his conservative allies celebrated the post-war conservatism of 1950s America and emphasized a return to traditionalism, presenting a nostalgic view of America before the tumult of the 1960s and 1970s. As Grateful Dead publicist Dennis McNally states in *Long Strange Trip*, "Ronald Reagan is president in the 80s and the great reaction had begun – the reaction against the 60s." President Reagan's successful campaign was designed to appeal to discouraged voters around the country and part of his methodology was denigrating 1960s counterculture, and its associated communities. As McNally states in *Long Strange Trip*, "Reagan ran as governor and president against the 1960s. And it worked." Reagan promoted a particular American lifestyle, and he juxtaposed and praised his version over that of alternative lifestyles like those practiced by the Deadheads.

After presenting the info above, distribute to learners a handout comparing and contrasting Reagan and Garcia: Handout-1---Ronald-Reagan-Jerry-Garcia.pdf (teachrock.wpenginepowered.com)

Give the class some time to read the two-page document. And then invite learners to take turns sharing one similarity and one difference they identified between Reagan and Garcia. The project manager is advised to write the responses on the board at the front of the classroom, organized into columns of

"Similarities" and "Differences." Save the responses to revisit and review later on. Next, have learners respond to the following:

- Noticing in particular the differences between Reagan and Garcia, might they have a different set of values that inform their individual lives?
- What might those values be?
- Might their supporters also have a different set of values?
- Could those who approve of Reagan's political views also support Garcia's artistic work?

Play for learners the clip, "Not the Band, but Deadheads": "Not the Band, but Deadheads" - TeachRock

Then have learners address the following:

- According to Grateful Dead publicist Dennis McNally, why did journalists first want to cover the Grateful Dead in the 1980s?
- At Grateful Dead concerts, what did journalists find to be more interesting than the band?
- Who are the Deadheads?
- How might the Deadheads be different from other fans of the Grateful Dead?
- Why might someone want to be a Deadhead?
- Considering the 1980s Deadheads seen in the clip, how might you characterize their community according to age, gender, economic status, etc.?
- Is it difficult to characterize Deadheads by this criteria? Why or why not?
- What might these characterizations say about Deadheads and the Grateful Dead in the 1980s?
- Might the Deadheads remind you of any other fan-group communities? If so, which ones? Might these groups share similar characteristics?

Day 4

Display for learners the 1980 Electoral College Map (of Reagan's landslide win), which can be located via search engine. Display the map for the class. Then have learners address the following:

- Looking at the image, which candidate won the election? How did you determine the winner? What do the numbers listed with each state signify?
- Did the winning candidate win by a significant amount in comparison to their opponent?
- Might candidate Ronald Reagan's victory lead you to conclude that voters supported his campaign themes and values over those of his opponent? Do you know any of those values?

Play for learners "Reagan's Radio Address to the Nation on the American Family": President Reagan's Radio Address to the Nation on the American Family - TeachRock

Then have learners address the following:

- What might President Reagan mean when he says that we may not be able to "go back to the old family ways"?
- What might those "family ways" be according to him?
- Do you think his version of "family ways" are the same as others'?
- Why might he be nostalgic for "the old family ways"?
- Why might President Reagan feel it necessary to "preserve family values"?

- How might his list of "family values" (faith, honesty, responsibility, tolerance, kindness, and love) contrast with those of the Deadheads?
- Might both Reagan and the Deadheads share some of those values? If so, which ones? Why?
- What might President Reagan mean when he says that his administration will keep "trying to create a better life for those who follow" those values?
- What particular groups of people might he be referring to as followers of those values?
- Might he be excluding those that don't "follow" those values? Might the Deadheads be excluded from the group of "those who follow" Reagan's values? If so, why?
- Considering President Reagan's address in total, how might his views contrast with those of the Deadheads that you just learned about in the previous video?
- Why might they contrast each other? What might be biasing your opinion?

Distribute to learners "The Television Family in the '80s": Handout-2-The-Television-Family-in-the-'80s.pdf (teachrock.wpenginepowered.com)

Organize learners into groups of two or three and have them discuss and answer the questions in the handout. Groups will need to select a scribe to jot the group's answers down. Once completed, ask groups to present their answers to the class. After group presentations of their thoughts, ideas, reactions to the document, have learners individually respond to the following:

- Do you think all of the families from these television shows followed the family values (faith, honesty, responsibility, tolerance, kindness, and love) President Reagan expressed in his radio address from 1984? If so, why? If not, why not?
- Do you think a family must identify as "conservative" like President Reagan did in order to follow these values? Can you think of groups that aren't families that may follow these values?

Day 5

The project manager is advised to explain to learners that the television show "Family Ties" was very popular in 1980s America. It depicted a nuclear family in which the mom and dad are liberal former counter culturalists who have become your typical suburban family. Their son, Alex P. Keaton, is depicted as a Young Republican "Yuppie." Explain that in the clip, Alex is on something comparable to Adderall: Family Ties - Sin Against Capitalism (youtube.com)

Then display for the class the cover to Marissa Piesman and Marlee Hartley's bestseller of the era, "The Yuppie Handbook: The State-of-the-Art Manual for Young Urban Professionals," which can be located via search engine. Explain to learners that the character Alex Keaton would proudly identify (and be labeled by society in the 1980s) as a Yuppie. Provide the background on the term by explaining that the term "Yuppie" was purposefully borrowed and modified from the 1960s counterculture term "Hippie" as a statement against the values of the counterculture i.e. those somewhat hypocritically espoused by Keaton's affluent parents). Then have learners respond to the following:

- What impressions might you get from this illustration of Yuppies?
- Their belongings are specifically labeled with brands — do you get the idea that these are the "right" or "ideal" things to do, own, wear, etc.? What would be considered the opposite?
- Might a Yuppie only be from a particular demographic? Can you list the characteristics of that demographic?
- Are we supposed to aspire to be like Yuppies? Why or why not?

- Why might the Deadheads want to reject this culture? Might it be possible to be a Deadhead and a Yuppie?
- Does the figure of the Yuppie exist today? If so, what characteristics might define them and how might they be similar or different than the Yuppies of the 1980s?

Next, play a clip where Jerry Garcia specifically comments on the Grateful Dead's fan culture during the 1980s and how the Deadhead experience of following the band on tour from show to show had a particular significance during this decade: "New Lame America" - TeachRock

Then have learners address the following:

- As the clip explains, the band's following in the 1980s began to include young people who weren't even alive during the Dead's early years. Why might Grateful Dead music and culture attract new fans in the 1980s?
- Why might these new fans in the 1980s become Deadheads and embrace the traditions of that particular community: following the Grateful Dead on tour, communing with other Deadheads and fans of the group, and attending as many shows as possible?
- How might the social and cultural norms promoted by President Reagan during the 1980s have influenced people to embrace alternative lifestyles and communities like the Deadheads?
- Might the appeal of these alternative lifestyles and communities contrast with Reagan's defined "family values"? Why or why not?
- What did Grateful Dead guitarist and vocalist Jerry Garcia think was appealing about the band? (Prompt learners to recognize that Garcia argued that the Grateful Dead cultural experience might offer an opportunity for "adventure.")
- Why might young people in the 1980s in particular have been looking for an adventure? Might their seeking of adventure have been influenced by President Reagan's promotion of "following" "family values"? Might it be possible to have an adventure and still follow those values?

Distribute to learners "Communing with the Dead": Handout-3-"Communing-with-the-Dead".pdf (teachrock.wpenginepowered.com)

Give the learners a few minutes to read the document and then a few minutes to respond to the following questions:

- Considering the content in the article and President Reagan's list of family values (faith, honesty, responsibility, tolerance, kindness, and love), might the author have been able to follow those values and also be a Deadhead? Why or why not?
- What particular aspect of the author's life noted in the article might conclude that she does follow those values?
- Considering the content in the article and the previously viewed video clip, "New Lame America," might it still be possible to have an "adventure" in America? What else was the author seeking with her journey besides an adventure?
- In what ways might the author view her Deadhead experience besides traveling the country to attend music concerts?
- Are there any other cultural traditions that you can think of that require someone to make a journey for specific purposes?
- Deadheads are still around today, but how do you think the Deadhead phenomenon would be covered in the news if it were new today? What similarities do you see between the cultural and political climate of today and the 1980s? How do Deadheads relate to today's "Stan" culture?

Day 6

Core Standards compel learners to write in a timed environment. To that end, learners are tasked with reading "My Disciplinarian Father, the Deadhead" My Disciplinarian Father, the Deadhead (melmagazine.com)

The project manager is advised to distribute the rubric (see Day 8):

Learners are then to write a short essay (with a thesis statement, body paragraph, and concluding statement) answering the following question: What do you take away from the article's portrait of Grateful Dead fandom, family and community, and how the values followed by the father in the article relate to Deadhead culture and President Reagan's promotion of family values?

Day 7

The project manager is advised to have learners review the rubric provided Day 6. Then, the project manager should present learners with the RADAR method of revision and encourage them to use some of the methods. Then provide them the period to revise their essays begun on Day 7. This essay must be posted to the Google Class stream by 11:59 pm tonight.

Day 8

Learners are to provide at least one peer review according to the following criteria:

Rubric

The peer reviewed here submitted their essay to the Google Class stream by 11:59 pm of Day 7. **(0-20 points)**

The peer's essay was free of spelling and grammar errors. **(0-10 points)**

The peer's essay had a clear a thesis statement that pertained to family values in both Regan's variant of American society and the Grateful Dead's variant of American society. **(0-10 points)**

The opening paragraph established the structure of the essay to follow. **(0-10 points)**

The first supporting paragraph addressed the question: What did the essayist peer reviewed here take away from the article's portrait of Grateful Dead fandom? **(0-10 points)**

The second supporting paragraph addressed the question: What the article's illuminates about family? **(0-10 points)**

What did the essayist peer reviewed here take away from the article's portrait of Grateful Dead fandom? **(0-10 points)**

The third supporting paragraph how the values followed by the father in the article relate to Deadhead culture and President Reagan's promotion of family values. **(0-10 points)**

The essay had a clear concluding statement. **(0-10 points)**

The conclusion of the essay also highlights some of the major points used as evidence to support the thesis statement (and rest of the essay). **(0-10 points)**

Total score _____

Made in United States
Troutdale, OR
06/03/2024